M000023481

ROMEO AND JULIET

WILLIAM SHAKESPEARE

WORKBOOK BY SUSANNAH WHITE

The right of Susannah White to be identified as the Author of this Work has been asserted by her in accordance with the Copyright, Designs and Patents Act 1988

YORK PRESS
322 Old Brompton Road, London SW5 9JH

PEARSON EDUCATION LIMITED
Edinburgh Gate, Harlow,
Essex CM20 2JE, United Kingdom
Associated companies, branches and representatives throughout the world

First published 2015

10 9 8 7 6 5

ISBN 978–1–2921–0082–1

Illustrations by Folko Streese; and Moreno Chiacchiera (page 54 only)

Typeset by Swales and Willis Ltd
Printed in Malaysia (CTP–PJB)

Photo credits: HHelene/Shutterstock for page 13 top / your/Shutterstock for page 15 top / Ralf Juergen Kraft/Shutterstock for page 17 top / Ivan Smuk/Shutterstock for page 19 top / Oksana Stepanova/Shutterstock for page 21 top / Robert B. Miller/Shutterstock for page 25 top / Dennis Jacobsen/Shutterstock for page 29 top / Aksenova Natalya/Shutterstock for page 35 bottom/ librakv/Shutterstock for page 49 bottom / underworld/Shutterstock for page 50 bottom / Boule/Shutterstock for page 51 top / Yingko/Shutterstock for page 60 top

CONTENTS

PART FOUR:
THEMES, CONTEXTS AND SETTINGS

PART FIVE:
FORM, STRUCTURE AND LANGUAGE

PART SIX:
PROGRESS BOOSTER ★

PART ONE: Getting Started

Preparing for assessment

HOW WILL I BE ASSESSED ON MY WORK ON *ROMEO AND JULIET*?

All exam boards are different, but whichever course you are following, your work will be examined through these four Assessment Objectives:

Assessment Objectives	Wording	Worth thinking about . . .
AO1	Read, understand and respond to texts. Students should be able to: • maintain a critical style and develop an informed personal response • use textual references, including quotations, to support and illustrate interpretations.	• How well do I know what happens, what people say, do, etc? • What do I think about the key ideas in the play? • How can I support my viewpoint in a really convincing way? • What are the best quotations to use and when should I use them?
AO2	Analyse the language, form and structure used by a writer to create meanings and effects, using relevant subject terminology where appropriate.	• What specific things does the writer 'do'? What choices has Shakespeare made? (Why this particular word, phrase or speech here? Why does this event happen at this point?) • What effects do these choices create? Suspense? Ironic laughter? Reflective mood?
AO3	Show understanding of the relationships between texts and the contexts in which they were written.	• What can I learn about society from the play? (What does it tell me about women in Shakespeare's day, for example?) • What was society like in Shakespeare's time? Can I see it reflected in the text?
AO4	Use a range of vocabulary and sentence structures for clarity, purpose and effect, with accurate spelling and punctuation.	• How accurately and clearly do I write? • Are there small errors of grammar, spelling and punctuation I can get rid of?

Look out for the Assessment Objective labels throughout your York Notes Workbook – these will help to focus your study and revision!

The text used in these Notes is the Penguin Shakespeare edition, 2005.

PART ONE: Getting Started

HOW TO USE YOUR YORK NOTES WORKBOOK

There are lots of ways your Workbook can support your study and revision of *Romeo and Juliet*. There is no 'right' way – choose the one that suits your learning style best.

1) Alongside the York Notes Study Guide and the text	2) As a 'stand-alone' revision programme	3) As a form of mock-exam
Do you have the York Notes Study Guide for *Romeo and Juliet*? The contents of your Workbook are designed to match the sections in the Study Guide, so with the play to hand you could: ● read the relevant section(s) of the Study Guide and any part of the play referred to ● complete the tasks in the same section in your Workbook.	Think you know *Romeo and Juliet* well? Why not work through the Workbook systematically, either as you finish scenes, or as you study or revise certain aspects in class or at home? You could make a revision diary and allocate particular sections of the Workbook to a day or week.	Prefer to do all your revision in one go? You could put aside a day or two and work through the Workbook, page by page. Once you have finished, check all your answers in one go! This will be quite a challenge, but it may be the approach you prefer.

HOW WILL THE WORKBOOK HELP YOU TEST AND CHECK YOUR KNOWLEDGE AND SKILLS?

Parts Two to **Five** offer a range of tasks and activities:

These fun and quick-to-complete tasks check your basic knowledge of the text

These more open questions challenge you to show your understanding

This task focuses on a key character, theme, technique, idea or relationship and helps you plan and write up paragraphs from an essay

A clear, quick way to record your progress visually

6 Romeo and Juliet

Each Part ends with a **Practice task** to extend your revision:

An exam-style task is provided at the end of each section for you to practise a full essay

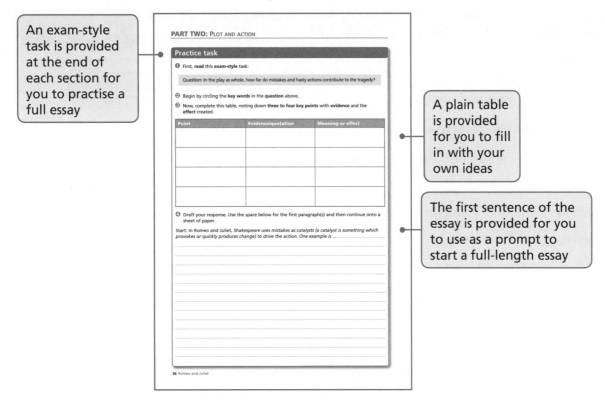

A plain table is provided for you to fill in with your own ideas

The first sentence of the essay is provided for you to use as a prompt to start a full-length essay

Part Six: Progress Booster helps you test your own key writing skills:

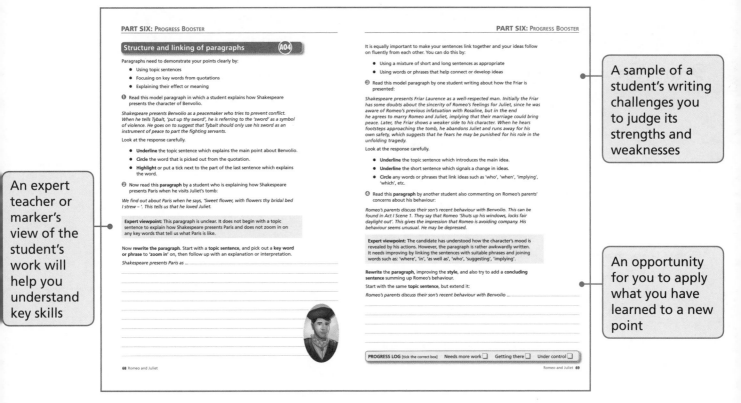

An expert teacher or marker's view of the student's work will help you understand key skills

A sample of a student's writing challenges you to judge its strengths and weaknesses

An opportunity for you to apply what you have learned to a new point

Don't forget – these are just some examples of the Workbook contents. Inside there is much more to help you revise. For example:

- lots of examples of students' own work at different levels
- help with spelling, punctuation and grammar
- advice and tasks on writing about context
- a full answer key so you can check your answers
- a full-length practice exam task with guidance on what to focus on.

PART TWO: PLOT AND ACTION

Act I Prologue and Scene 1: Establishing the conflict

QUICK TEST ✔

❶ **Tick** the box for the **correct answer** to each of these questions:

a) When does the Prologue suggest that the feud will finally end?

when the lovers die ☐   after a street fight ☐   when the Prince demands peace ☐

b) Who is Romeo in love with at the start of the play?

Juliet ☐   Rosaline ☐   Mab ☐

c) What punishment does the Prince suggest for anybody who fights again?

banishment ☐   death ☐   imprisonment ☐

d) Which poetic form is the Prologue written in?

ballad ☐   sonnet ☐   free verse ☐

e) Who expresses the bittersweet nature of love though the use of oxymorons?

Benvolio ☐   Romeo ☐   Sampson ☐

THINKING MORE DEEPLY ?

❷ Write **one** or **two sentences** in response to each of these questions:

a) What is the dramatic significance of the street fight?

....

....

....

....

b) How are the attitudes of Benvolio and Tybalt different?

....

....

....

....

c) What is Benvolio talking about when he says, 'I'll know his grievance or be much denied.' (I.1.157)?

....

....

....

....

EXAM PREPARATION: WRITING ABOUT THE PRINCE **A01**

Reread the section from *'Rebellious subjects ...'* (l.1.81) to *'all men depart.'* (l.1.103)

Question: How does the Prince react to the feud?

Think about:

- The words he uses
- The punishment he suggests

❸ Complete this table

Point/Detail	Evidence	Effect or explanation
1: *The Prince thinks the families' behaviour is unacceptable.*	*'Rebellious subjects, enemies to peace,'* (l.1.81)	*The adjective 'rebellious' suggests that the families are opposing the state; 'enemies' makes us think of war, adding to the violent tone.*
2: *He condemns their frequent street fights.*		
3: *He threatens to punish them.*		

❹ Write up **point 1** into a **paragraph** below in your own words. Remember to include what you infer from the evidence, or the writer's effects:

....

....

....

....

....

❺ Now, choose **one** of your **other points** and write it out as another **paragraph** here:

....

....

....

....

....

....

PROGRESS LOG [tick the correct box]   Needs more work ☐   Getting there ☐   Under control ☐

Act I Scene 2: Juliet's future in the balance

QUICK TEST

❶ **Number** the events of this section so that they are in the **correct sequence**.
Use 1 for the first event and 6 for the final event:

a) Capulet suggests that Juliet is too young to marry.	
b) A servant is sent out to deliver invitations to the ball.	
c) Romeo decides to go to the ball.	
d) Paris asks Lord Capulet for Juliet's hand in marriage.	
e) Capulet reveals that he is planning to hold a ball that night and he invites Paris.	
f) Romeo sees that Rosaline is on the guest list.	

THINKING MORE DEEPLY

❷ Write **one** or **two sentences** in response to each of these questions:

a) What impression do the audience get of Paris from his conversation with Lord Capulet?

....

....

....

b) What is the dramatic significance of Romeo's meeting with the servant?

....

....

....

c) In what way does Shakespeare use these scenes to 'plant the seeds' of some of the troubles that happen later in the play?

....

....

....

EXAM PREPARATION: WRITING ABOUT LORD CAPULET

Reread the section from *'But now my Lord, what say you to my suit?'* (I.2.6) to *'makes my number more.'* (I.2.23)

Question: What is Lord Capulet's attitude to Paris's marriage proposal?

Think about:

- The way Capulet speaks about Juliet
- The way he responds to Paris

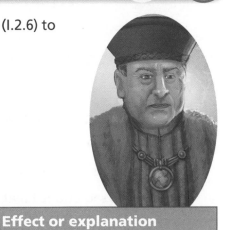

❸ Complete this table

Point/Detail	Evidence	Effect or explanation
1: *Lord Capulet is worried that Juliet may be too young for marriage.*	*'My child is yet a stranger to this world;'* (I.2.8)	*The word 'stranger' suggests that she needs more time to experience life before she marries.*
2: *He is willing to consider Juliet's opinion.*		
3: *Capulet hopes that Paris can win Juliet's heart.*		

❹ Write up **point 1** into a **paragraph** below in your own words. Remember to include what you infer from the evidence, or the writer's effects:

....

....

....

....

❺ Now, choose **one** of your **other points** and write it out as another **paragraph** here:

....

....

....

....

PROGRESS LOG [tick the correct box]   Needs more work ☐   Getting there ☐   Under control ☐

Act I Scenes 3 and 4: Marriage and misgivings

QUICK TEST ✔

❶ Which of these are **TRUE** statements and which are **FALSE**? Write **'T'** or **'F'** in the boxes:

a) Lady Capulet does not want Juliet to marry. ☐

b) Juliet is willing to consider Paris's proposal. ☐

c) The Nurse is a quiet character. ☐

d) Romeo is sad about Juliet. ☐

e) The Nurse refers to the physical aspects of love. ☐

f) Juliet seems to be closer to her mother than to the Nurse. ☐

g) Romeo feels fearful about the future. ☐

THINKING MORE DEEPLY ✔

❷ Write **one** or **two sentences** in response to each of these questions:

a) What does Lady Capulet mean when she says, 'So shall you share all that he doth possess / By having him, making yourself no less.' (I.3.95)?

b) How does the Nurse annoy Lady Capulet?

c) How does Mercutio respond to Romeo's depression?

EXAM PREPARATION: WRITING ABOUT ROMEO'S INFATUATION (A02)

Reread the section from *'Give me a torch...'* (I.4.11) to *'pricks like thorn.'* (I.4.26)

Question: How does Shakespeare show that Romeo's infatuation with Rosaline is making him suffer?

Think about:

- What Romeo says
- How he responds to his friends

❸ Complete this table

Point/Detail	Evidence	Effect or explanation
1: *Romeo feels depressed.*	*'Being but heavy, I will bear the light.'* (I.4.12)	*The use of the word 'heavy' shows that Romeo feels burdened. It contrasts with 'light', which conveys luminosity and brightness.*
2: *He refuses to dance.*		
3: *He describes the pain of love.*		

❹ Write up **point 1** into a **paragraph** below in your own words. Remember to include what you infer from the evidence, or the writer's effects:

....

....

....

....

❺ Now, choose **one** of your **other points** and write it out as another **paragraph** here:

....

....

....

....

....

PROGRESS LOG [tick the correct box]   Needs more work ☐   Getting there ☐   Under control ☐

Act I Scene 5: Romeo and Juliet meet

QUICK TEST

❶ Complete **this gap-fill paragraph** about the scene, with the **correct or suitable information:**

This scene is set at Lord Capulet's ball. Capulet's nephew, Tybalt, feels .... because

Romeo is at the party. Capulet does not want Tybalt to .... the party and warns him not

to make a .... amongst his .... He tells Tybalt that he must be .... and not

challenge Romeo on such an occasion. This shows that Capulet cares about his ....

in this context whereas Tybalt always wants to fight with the Montagues, whatever the situation

and consequences are.

THINKING MORE DEEPLY

❷ Write **one** or **two sentences** in response to each of these questions:

a) How do we know that Capulet is aware of some of Romeo's positive traits?

....

....

....

....

....

....

b) How does Shakespeare show us that Romeo finds Juliet beautiful?

....

....

....

....

....

....

c) How and why does Juliet's mood change at the end of this scene?

....

....

....

....

....

EXAM PREPARATION: WRITING ABOUT LOVE

Reread the section from *'If I profane ...'* (line 93) to *'my prayer's effect I take.'* (line 106)

Question: How does Shakespeare convey Romeo and Juliet's love in this shared sonnet?

Think about:

- The way they interact
- The imagery Shakespeare uses

❸ Complete this table

Point/Detail	Evidence	Effect or explanation
1: *Romeo and Juliet mirror each other's language.*	*Juliet: 'And palm to palm is holy palmers' kiss.'* *Romeo: 'Have not saints lips, and holy palmers too?' (lines 100–1)*	*The way that they repeat each other's language creates a sense of harmony, for example in the repetition of 'palmers' and the linked 'kiss' and 'lips'.*
2: *Shakespeare uses religious imagery.*		
3: *Romeo shows his devotion to Juliet.*		

❹ Write up **point 1** into a **paragraph** below in your own words. Remember to include what you infer from the evidence, or the writer's effects:

....

....

....

....

....

❺ Now, choose **one** of your other points and write it out as another **paragraph** here:

....

....

....

....

....

PROGRESS LOG [tick the correct box]   Needs more work ☐   Getting there ☐   Under control ☐

Act II Prologue and Scene 1: More about Romeo

QUICK TEST ✓

❶ Which of these are **TRUE** statements and which are **FALSE**? Write **'T'** or **'F'** in the boxes:

a) The sombre tone of the Prologue contrasts with the liveliness of Capulet's ball. ☐

b) This second Prologue is not a sonnet. ☐

c) The Chorus explain that Romeo's infatuation with Rosaline is over. ☐

d) Mercutio and Benvolio know that Romeo is in love with Juliet. ☐

e) Mercutio refers to love by using sexual innuendos. ☐

f) Mercutio saw Romeo jump over the orchard wall. ☐

THINKING MORE DEEPLY ?

❷ Write **one** or **two sentences** in response to each of these questions:

a) What does Romeo mean when he says, 'Can I go forward when my heart is here?' (II.1.15)

....

....

....

....

....

....

b) How do we know that Benvolio is concerned about Romeo?

....

....

....

....

....

....

c) What reasons does Mercutio have to call Romeo a 'Madman!' (II.1.7)?

....

....

....

....

....

....

EXAM PREPARATION: WRITING ABOUT THE PROLOGUE

Reread the Prologue to Act II.

Question: What is the dramatic and thematic significance of the Act II Prologue?

Think about:

- The feelings it describes
- The indications it gives about the future

❸ Complete this table

Point/Detail	Evidence	Effect or explanation
1: *The Prologue reminds the audience that Romeo's feelings have changed.*	*'Old desire doth in his deathbed lie,' (line 1)*	*Romeo's infatuation is personified as a dying person. The use of the word 'deathbed' foreshadows future events.*
2: *It sets the scene for future difficulties.*		
3: *It shows the strength of Romeo and Juliet's love.*		

❹ Write up **point 1** into a **paragraph** below in your own words. Remember to include what you infer from the evidence, or the writer's effects:

....
....
....
....
....

❺ Now, choose one of your **other points** and write it out as another **paragraph** here:

....
....
....
....
....

PROGRESS LOG [tick the correct box]   Needs more work ☐   Getting there ☐   Under control ☐

Act II Scene 2: The tender meeting of the lovers

QUICK TEST

❶ **Number** the events of this section so that they are in the **correct sequence**. Use 1 for the first event and 6 for the final event:

a) Romeo sees Juliet at her window.	
b) Juliet is embarrassed because Romeo has heard what she said.	
c) Juliet declares her love for Romeo and Romeo overhears her.	
d) The couple exchange vows of love.	
e) Juliet asks Romeo to arrange their marriage.	
f) Romeo has climbed over the orchard wall.	

THINKING MORE DEEPLY

❷ Write **one** or **two sentences** in response to each of these questions:

a) What sources of light are mentioned between lines 2 and 25 and what is their significance?

....

....

....

....

b) What will Juliet gain from a quick marriage?

....

....

....

....

c) What is Juliet thinking about when she says, 'That which we call a rose / By any other name would smell as sweet' (lines 43–4)?

....

....

....

....

EXAM PREPARATION: WRITING ABOUT DANGER  A02

Reread the section from *'With love's light wings ...'* (line 66) to *'within my breast.'* (line 124).

Question: How does Shakespeare convey a sense of danger in this scene?

Think about:

- Juliet's fears
- The timing of Romeo's visit

❸ Complete this table

Point/Detail	Evidence	Effect or explanation
1: *Juliet's family would kill Romeo if they saw him.*	*'If they do see thee, they will murder thee.'* (line 70)	*Romeo's life is in danger because the lovers come from rival families.*
2: *Romeo has to visit Juliet at night.*		
3: *Juliet worries about the speed of their relationship.*		

❹ Write up **point 1** into a **paragraph** below in your own words. Remember to include what you infer from the evidence, or the writer's effects:

....

....

....

....

❺ Now, choose **one** of your other points and write it out as another **paragraph** here:

....

....

....

....

....

PROGRESS LOG [tick the correct box]   Needs more work ☐   Getting there ☐   Under control ☐

Act II Scenes 3 and 4: Making plans

QUICK TEST ✔

❶ **Tick** the box for the **correct answer** to each of these questions:

a) What is the Friar carrying when the audience first see him?

rosary beads ☐   a Bible ☐   herbs ☐

b) What does the Friar hope that the marriage between Romeo and Juliet will bring?

wealth ☐   peace ☐   gifts ☐

c) What has Tybalt sent to Romeo?

poison ☐   a challenge ☐   a dagger ☐

d) How does Mercutio behave towards the Nurse?

he teases her ☐   he confronts her ☐   he ignores her ☐

e) What does Romeo arrange with the Nurse?

a street fight ☐   a masked ball ☐   his wedding ☐

THINKING MORE DEEPLY ❓

❷ Write **one** or **two sentences** in response to each of these questions:

a) What is the Friar's opinion of young lovers?

....

....

....

....

b) How does Shakespeare suggest that Romeo often confides in the Friar?

....

....

....

....

c) What does Mercutio mean when he says, 'Now art thou sociable. Now art thou Romeo.' (II.4.87)?

....

....

....

....

EXAM PREPARATION: WRITING ABOUT LIFE AND DEATH

Reread the section from *'Now, ere the sun ....'* (II.3.1) to *'death eats up the plant.'* (II.3.26)

Question: How does Shakespeare use this speech by the Friar to explore the theme of life and death?

Think about:

- The language he uses
- The herbs the Friar speaks about

❸ Complete this table

Point/Detail	Evidence	Effect or explanation
1: *The Friar uses words related to birth in relation to the natural world.*	*'mother' and 'womb' (I.3.5–6)*	*Since life begins in a mother's womb, these words suggest the idea of a baby being born.*
2: *He also uses words with connotations of death.*		
3: *The Friar suggests that herbs can cure or kill.*		

❹ Write up **point 1** into a **paragraph** below in your own words. Remember to include what you infer from the evidence, or the writer's effects:

....

....

....

....

....

❺ Now, choose **one** of your **other points** and write it out as another **paragraph** here:

....

....

....

....

....

....

PROGRESS LOG [tick the correct box]   Needs more work ☐   Getting there ☐   Under control ☐

Act II Scenes 5 and 6: Waiting and a wedding

QUICK TEST ✔

❶ Complete **this gap-fill paragraph** about the scene, with the **correct or suitable information:**

Juliet is anxious about the passing of .... She is waiting impatiently for the Nurse to bring her .... from Romeo. Juliet is alone on stage as the scene begins, so her speech is a .... She speaks about 'love's ....' and how they should travel as fast as the flickering of the .... when clouds pass over it. This image connects to the theme of .... in the play.

THINKING MORE DEEPLY ❓

❷ Write **one** or **two sentences** in response to each of these questions:

a) What kind of relationship does the Juliet have with the Nurse?

....
....
....
....
....
....

b) How can we infer that Juliet is impatient to hear news from Romeo?

....
....
....
....
....
....

c) What does the Friar mean when he says, 'violent delights have violent ends' (II.6.9)?

....
....
....
....
....

EXAM PREPARATION: WRITING ABOUT THE NURSE   **A01**

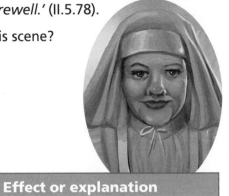

Reread the section from *'I am aweary ....'* (II.5.25) to *'Honest Nurse, farewell.'* (II.5.78).

Question: What impression does Shakespeare give of the Nurse in this scene?

Think about:

- What she talks about
- How she behaves

❸ Complete this table

Point/Detail	Evidence	Effect or explanation
1: *Shakespeare suggests that the Nurse is physically weak.*	*'I am a weary' (line 25)*	*The Nurse is old and her journey has made her tired, contrasting with the vivacity of youth.*
2: *She seems in no hurry to deliver her news. This implies that she does not fully understand the strength of Juliet's love for Romeo.*		
3: *She does want to help Juliet.*		

❹ Write up **point 1** into a **paragraph** below in your own words. Remember to include what you infer from the evidence, or the writer's effects:

....

....

....

....

....

❺ Now, choose **one** of your other points and write it out as another **paragraph** here:

....

....

....

....

....

PROGRESS LOG [tick the correct box]   Needs more work ☐   Getting there ☐   Under control ☐

Act III Scene 1: A fatal fight

QUICK TEST ✓

❶ Write the correct names by each quotation to show **who is speaking and about whom**:

Some names are used more than once.

Romeo   Juliet   Mercutio   Tybalt   Benvolio   The Prince

a) 'I do protest I never injured thee ...' (III.1.67) Said by: .... about ....

b) 'Good King of Cats' (III.1.75) Said by: .... about ....

c) 'Thy beauty hath made me effeminate,' (III.1.114) Said by: .... about ....

d) 'Thou, wretched boy, ...' (III.1.130) Said by: .... about ....

e) 'There lies the man, slain by young Romeo,' (III.1.144) Said by: .... about ....

f) 'Immediately we do exile him hence.' (III.1.187) Said by: .... about ....

THINKING MORE DEEPLY ?

❷ Write **one** or **two** sentences in response to each of these questions.

a) How can we tell that Benvolio is worried at the start of this scene?

....

....

....

....

b) What is Romeo's initial attitude to Tybalt's challenge?

....

....

....

....

c) What does Mercutio mean when he says, 'Ask for me / tomorrow, and you shall find me a grave man.' (III.1.99)?

....

....

....

....

EXAM PREPARATION: WRITING ABOUT STRUCTURE	A02

Reread the section from line 136 *'O, I am fortune's fool ...'* to line 197 *'pardoning those that kill.'*

Question: Why is Act III Scene 1 a turning point in the play?

Think about:

- The consequences of this scene for Romeo

❸ Complete this table

Point/Detail	Evidence	Effect or explanation
1: Romeo's hasty actions have changed his future.	'O, I am fortune's fool!' (line 136).	Romeo realises what he has done and believes he is a victim of fate, echoing the Prologue's reference to 'star-crossed lovers.'
2: His mistake must be punished.		
3: His punishment means that he will never be able to return to Verona.		

❹ Write up **point 1** into a **paragraph** below in your own words. Remember to include what you infer from the evidence, or the writer's effects:

....

....

....

....

....

❺ Now, choose **one** of your other points and write it out as another **paragraph** here:

....

....

....

....

....

PROGRESS LOG [tick the correct box]	Needs more work ☐	Getting there ☐	Under control ☐

Act III Scenes 2 and 3: Dealing with the consequences

QUICK TEST ✔

❶ Which of these are **TRUE** statements about this section, and which are **FALSE**?
Write 'T' or 'F' in the boxes:

a) The Nurse tells Juliet that Romeo has killed Tybalt.   ☐

b) The Nurse forbids Juliet to see Romeo again.   ☐

c) The Friar tells Romeo that he is banished from Verona.   ☐

d) Juliet is too upset to see Romeo.   ☐

e) Romeo wants to kill himself.   ☐

f) The Friar suggests that Romeo should go to Venice.   ☐

g) Romeo often turns to the Friar for help.   ☐

THINKING MORE DEEPLY ?

❷ Write **one** or **two sentences** in response to each of these questions:

a) How does the Nurse help Juliet?

....

....

....

....

....

b) How does Shakespeare convey Juliet's confusion about Tybalt's death?

....

....

....

....

....

c) What is Romeo's attitude to his punishment?

....

....

....

....

EXAM PREPARATION: WRITING ABOUT THE FRIAR

Reread the section from *'Hold thy desperate hand…'* (III.3.108) to *'Romeo is coming'* (III.3.158).

Question: How does the Friar comfort Romeo in this scene?

Think about:

- How he offers Romeo hope
- What he says about Juliet

❸ Complete this table

Point/Detail	Evidence	Effect or explanation
1: *The Friar stops Romeo from killing himself. However, this intervention just delays Romeo's inevitable death as foretold in the Prologue.*	*'Wilt thou slay thyself? / And slay thy lady that in thy life lives,'* (lines 116–17)	*The Friar suggests that Romeo is being hasty and selfish by not thinking about Juliet.*
2: *He tells Romeo to visit Juliet.*		
3: *The Friar suggests that the Prince might forgive Romeo.*		

❹ Write up **point 1** into a **paragraph** below in your own words. Remember to include what you infer from the evidence, or the writer's effects:

....

....

....

....

....

❺ Now, choose **one** of your other points and write it out as another **paragraph** here:

....

....

....

....

....

PROGRESS LOG [tick the correct box]   Needs more work ☐   Getting there ☐   Under control ☐

Act III Scenes 4 and 5: A plan and a parting

① **Number** the events of this section so that they are in the correct sequence. Use 1 for the first event and 7 for the final event:

a) Lady Capulet tells Juliet she must marry Romeo.	
b) The lovers wake and realise that it is day.	
c) The Nurse arrives with news that Lady Capulet is on her way to see Juliet.	
d) Romeo and Juliet part hastily.	
e) Juliet refuses to marry Paris.	
f) Lord Capulet insists Juliet must marry Paris or be disinherited.	
g) The Capulets decide that Juliet should marry Paris.	

② Write **one** or **two sentences** in response to each of these questions:

a) What is the real cause of Juliet's distress?

....

....

....

....

b) How does Capulet show the strength of his feelings when Juliet defies him?

....

....

....

....

c) How does the Nurse betray Juliet?

....

....

....

....

EXAM PREPARATION: WRITING ABOUT THE LOVERS

Reread the section from *'Wilt thou be gone?'* (III.5.1) to *'I'll descend.'* (III.5.42).

Question: How do the two young lovers react to the prospect of parting?

Think about:

- The language they use
- Their reactions to each other

❸ Complete this table

Point/Detail	Evidence	Effect or explanation
1: *Juliet tries to deny that it is morning but Romeo corrects her.*	*Juliet: 'It was the nightingale and not the lark,' (III.5.2)* *Romeo: 'It was the lark, the herald of the morn;' (III.5.6)*	*Juliet attempts to halt time to spend longer with Romeo, but he brings her back to reality.*
2: *Romeo is willing to face danger in order to stay with Juliet.*		
3: *Juliet does not want Romeo to stay and be hurt.*		

❹ Write up **point 1** into a **paragraph** below in your own words. Remember to include what you infer from the evidence, or the writer's effects:

....

....

....

....

....

❺ Now, choose one of your **other points** and write it out as another **paragraph** here:

....

....

....

....

....

PROGRESS LOG [tick the correct box]   Needs more work ☐   Getting there ☐   Under control ☐

Act IV Scenes 1 and 2: Plans and preparations

QUICK TEST ?

❶ Write the correct names by each quotation to show **who is speaking and about whom**:

Some of the names are used more than once.

Friar   Juliet   Capulet   Paris

a) 'Thy face is mine, and thou hast slandered it.' (IV.I.35) Said by: .... about ....

b) 'On Thursday next be married to this County.' (IV.I.49) Said by: .... about ....

c) 'Hold, daughter. I do spy a kind of hope,' (IV.I.68) Said by: .... about ....

d) 'Henceforward I am ever ruled by you' (IV.2.22). Said by: .... about ....

e) 'All our whole city is much bound to him' (IV.2.32) Said by: .... about ....

f) 'Since this same wayward girl is so reclaimed' (IV.2.47) Said by: .... about ....

THINKING MORE DEEPLY ?

❷ Write **one** or **two sentences** in response to each of these questions:

a) How does Paris treat Juliet?

....

....

....

....

b) What is Lady Capulet worried about when she says, 'We shall be short in our provision.' (IV.2.38)?

....

....

....

....

c) What makes Lord Capulet claim that his 'heart is wondrous light,' (IV.2.46)?

....

....

....

....

....

EXAM PREPARATION: WRITING ABOUT JULIET

Reread the section from *'O shut the door ...'* (IV.I.44) to *'wife to my sweet love.'* (IV.I.88).

Question: What impression does Shakespeare give of Juliet in this extract?

Think about:

- Her actions

- The language that she uses

❸ Complete this table

Point/Detail	Evidence	Effect or explanation
1: *Shakespeare suggests that Juliet is desperate.*	*'And with this knife I'll help it presently.' (line 54)*	*Her rash actions mirror Romeo's since he also wanted to kill himself at a time of difficulty.*
2: *She is prepared to face any danger to avoid marrying Paris.*		
3: *Juliet has moral concerns about a second marriage.*		

❹ Write up **point 1** into a **paragraph** below in your own words. Remember to include what you infer from the evidence, or the writer's effects:

....

....

....

....

....

....

❺ Now, choose **one** of your other points and write it out as another **paragraph** here:

....

....

....

....

....

....

PROGRESS LOG [tick the correct box]　　Needs more work ☐　　Getting there ☐　　Under control ☐

Act IV Scenes 3, 4 and 5: The potion ends the wedding plans

QUICK TEST ✓

❶ Which of these are **TRUE** statements and which are **FALSE**?
Write '**T**' or '**F**' in the boxes:

a) Juliet's speech about taking the potion is a soliloquy. ☐

b) Juliet takes the potion because of her grief over Tybalt. ☐

c) She is afraid of seeing corpses and skeletons in the tomb. ☐

d) She shows courage and resilience when she takes the potion. ☐

e) Lord and Lady Capulet are busy arranging Tybalt's funeral. ☐

f) Lady Capulet is the first to find Juliet and thinks that she is dead. ☐

g) The Prince agrees to arrange Juliet's funeral. ☐

THINKING MORE DEEPLY ?

❷ Write **one** or **two sentences** in response to each of these questions:

a) How can we infer that Juliet is anxious about taking the potion?

....
....
....
....
....

b) What is the purpose of the comic interlude at the end of Act IV?

....
....
....
....
....

c) How do Juliet's parents and the Nurse express their grief?

....
....
....
....
....

EXAM PREPARATION: WRITING ABOUT THE FRIAR'S BEHAVIOUR

Reread the section from *'Peace, ho, for shame ...'* (IV.5.65) to *'reason's merriment.'* (IV.5.83).

Question: How does Shakespeare present the Friar's behaviour in this scene?

Think about:

- What he says
- What the audience know but the Capulet family do not

❸ Complete this table

Point/Detail	Evidence	Effect or explanation
1: *Shakespeare shows how the Friar stops Juliet's family from expressing their grief.*	*'Peace, ho, for shame!' (IV.5.65)*	*He has no reason to grieve, as he knows Juliet is still alive. Their grief may be upsetting him or even making him feel guilty.*
2: *The Friar appears to reassure Capulet that he should not blame himself for Juliet's death.*		
3: *He claims that Juliet is in heaven but the audience know he is lying.*		

❹ Write up **point 1** into a **paragraph** below in your own words. Remember to include what you infer from the evidence, or the writer's effects:

....

....

....

....

....

....

❺ Now, choose **one** of your other points and write it out as another **paragraph** here:

....

....

....

....

....

....

....

PROGRESS LOG [tick the correct box]　　Needs more work ☐　　Getting there ☐　　Under control ☐

Act V Scenes 1, 2 and 3: The tragedy unfolds

❶ **Tick** the box for the **correct answer** to each of these questions:

a) Who tells Romeo that Juliet is dead?

The Friar ☐   Benvolio ☐   Balthasar ☐

b) Where does Romeo go first when he hears that Juliet is dead?

Verona ☐   the tomb ☐   to see an apothecary ☐

c) Who tells Friar Laurence that his message was not delivered?

Balthasar ☐   Benvolio ☐   Friar John ☐

d) What do both the Friar and the Apothecary provide in the play?

advice ☐   blessings ☐   potions ☐

e) Who does Romeo send away from the tomb?

Balthasar ☐   Paris ☐   the Friar ☐

f) What does the Friar do when he hears people approaching the tomb?

confess ☐   run away ☐   fight them ☐

❷ Write **one** or **two sentences** in response to each of these questions:

a) What impression does Shakespeare give of Paris in Act V?

....

....

....

....

b) What does the Prince mean when he says 'all are punished' (V.3.295)?

....

....

....

....

c) How does the idea of a 'glooming peace' (V.3.305) connect to the play's themes?

....

....

....

....

EXAM PREPARATION: WRITING ABOUT ROMEO IN THE TOMB

Reread the section from *'For here lies Juliet ...'* (V.3.85) to *'Thus with a kiss I die.'* (V.3.120).

Question: How does Romeo react to the sight of Juliet lying in the tomb?

Think about:

- The language he uses
- His actions

❸ Complete this table

Point/Detail	Evidence	Effect or explanation
1: *Romeo uses an image of light to describe Juliet.*	*'For here lies Juliet, and her beauty makes / This vault a feasting presence full of light.'* (lines 85–6)	*Death is usually connected to darkness but Romeo refers to Juliet's beauty as illuminating, as he has done throughout the play.*
2: *He claims that Death has not diminished her beauty.*		
3: *Romeo wishes to die in order to join Juliet.*		

❹ Write up **point 1** into a **paragraph** below in your own words. Remember to include what you infer from the evidence, or the writer's effects:

....

....

....

....

....

❺ Now, choose **one** of your other points and write it out as another **paragraph** here:

....

....

....

....

....

....

PROGRESS LOG [tick the correct box]   Needs more work ☐   Getting there ☐   Under control ☐

Practice task

❶ First, **read** this **exam-style** task:

Question: In the play as whole, how far do mistakes and hasty actions contribute to the tragedy?

❷ Begin by circling the **key words** in the **question** above.

❸ Now, complete this table, noting down **three to four key points** with **evidence** and the **effect** created.

Point	Evidence/quotation	Meaning or effect

❹ Draft your response. Use the space below for the first paragraph(s) and then continue onto a sheet of paper.

Start: *In* Romeo and Juliet, *Shakespeare uses mistakes as catalysts (a catalyst is something which provokes or quickly produces change) to drive the action. One example is ...*

PART THREE: CHARACTERS

Who's who?

Look at these drawings and complete the name of each of the characters shown.

.... Montague

.... Capulet

Lord and Lady ....

Lord and Lady ....

Friar ....

....................., Romeo's friend

....................., Juliet's cousin

....................., killed by Tybalt

The ....

Romeo

❶ Look at these statements about Romeo and decide whether they are **True [T]**, **False [F]** or whether there is **Not Enough Evidence [NEE]** to make a decision.

a) At the start of the play Romeo is infatuated with Rosaline.   [T] [F] [NEE]

b) Shakespeare uses oxymorons to convey Romeo's infatuation.   [T] [F] [NEE]

c) Romeo loved many women before Juliet.   [T] [F] [NEE]

d) Romeo's parents are concerned about him.   [T] [F] [NEE]

e) Romeo has a good reputation in Verona.   [T] [F] [NEE]

f) Romeo is given the death penalty after he kills Tybalt.   [T] [F] [NEE]

g) Romeo kills the Prince at the tomb.   [T] [F] [NEE]

❷ Complete each of these **statements** about Romeo, using **your own words:**

a) From the start of the play, we can infer that Romeo thinks a lot about ... .

....

b) When he speaks about his love for Juliet he uses ... .

....

c) When he needs help, he turns to the Friar because ... .

....

d) Romeo's main weakness is that he ... .

....

e) His total devotion to Juliet is demonstrated by ... .

....

❸ Using your own **judgement** put a mark along this line to show **Shakespeare's overall presentation** of Romeo based on what you have read:

Not at all sympathetic	A little sympathetic	Quite sympathetic	Very sympathetic
❶	❷	❸	❹

PROGRESS LOG [tick the correct box]   Needs more work ☐   Getting there ☐   Under control ☐

Juliet

❶ Each of these qualities could be applied to Juliet. Working from **memory,** add points from the play when you think she shows them, then find at least one **quotation** to back up your ideas.

Quality	Moments in play	Quotation
a) obedient		
b) impatient		
c) brave		
d) loyal		

❷ Look at the words spoken by Juliet as she prepares to take the Friar's potion. Add **further annotations** to them, using suitable adjectives from the bank at the bottom of the page, and explain how Shakespeare's words help to convey Juliet's character.

'My dismal scene I needs must <u>act alone</u>.

Come, vial.

What if this mixture do not work at all?

Shall I be married then tomorrow morning?

No, no! This shall forbid it. Lie thou there.' (IV.3.19–21)

the word 'alone' shows that she feels isolated

anxious	*devoted*	*sensitive*	*intelligent*
determined	*impatient*	*resourceful*	*isolated*

PROGRESS LOG [tick the correct box]   Needs more work ☐   Getting there ☐   Under control ☐

Mercutio

❶ Look at this bank of **adjectives** describing Mercutio. Circle the ones you think best **describe** him:

lively	*witty*	*imaginative*
calm	*light-hearted*	*cowardly*
quick-tempered	*quiet*	*talkative*
energetic *sensitive*	*bawdy*	*shy*

❷ Now add a **scene reference** from your copy of the play next to each circle, showing where evidence can be found to **support** the **adjective.**

❸ Complete this **gap-fill paragraph** about Mercutio, adding the **correct information**:

Mercutio is one of Romeo's close .... He provides humour in

the play as his lines are full of .... His 'Queen Mab' speech

shows the .... side of his character. However, Mercutio is not

always in a light-hearted mood. He can also be violent and he feels very

.... when Romeo refuses to fight with Tybalt. Benvolio tries

to persuade him to avoid conflict, but Mercutio .... his friend's

warning. Mercutio's .... is a significant point in the play.

❹ Write **one** or **two sentences** in response to this question: What are the effects of Mercutio's death?

....

....

....

....

....

....

....

....

....

....

PROGRESS LOG [tick the correct box]   Needs more work ☐   Getting there ☐   Under control ☐

The Nurse

❶ Complete these quotations **describing** or **said by** the Nurse:

a) 'Thou wast the prettiest babe that e'er I ....' (I.3.61)

b) 'Enough of this. I pray thee hold thy ....' (I.3.50)

c) 'O, she is ....! Love's heralds should be thoughts,' (II.5.4)

d) 'I am ....Give me leave a while.' (II.5.25)

e) 'I think it best you married with the ....' (III.5.217)

f) 'She's dead, deceased. She's dead .... the day!' (IV.5.22)

❷ Write **one** or **two** sentences in response to each of these questions:

a) In what ways does Shakespeare use the Nurse to add humour to the play?

....

....

....

....

....

b) How does Juliet's relationship with the Nurse change?

....

....

....

....

....

❸ Write a **paragraph** explaining how **Shakespeare presents** the Nurse. Try to use one of the quotations above, or another of your choice to **support** what you say: *believe Shakespeare presents the Nurse as ...* ....

....

....

....

....

....

PROGRESS LOG [tick the correct box]   Needs more work ☐   Getting there ☐   Under control ☐

Friar Laurence

❶ Read these statements about the Friar and decide whether they are **True [T]**, **False [F]** or whether there is **Not Enough Evidence [NEE]** to make a decision.

a) The Friar is a skilled herbalist.   [T] [F] [NEE]

b) He hopes that Romeo and Juliet's marriage will end the feud. [T] [F] [NEE]

c) He refuses to leave Juliet alone in the tomb.   [T] [F] [NEE]

d) Shakespeare portrays the Friar in a wholly positive light.   [T] [F] [NEE]

e) The Friar has made many previous attempts to end the feud. [T] [F] [NEE]

f) The Prince does not punish him at the end of the play.   [T] [F] [NEE]

❷ Complete these **statements** about the Friar using **your own words**.

a) *Friar Laurence is a man of holy orders who agrees to marry Romeo and Juliet because he ...*

....

....

b) *Later in the play, he makes further plans to support Romeo and Juliet by ...*

....

....

c) *His plans go wrong when ...*

....

....

d) *He shows that he has a cowardly side when he ...*

....

....

e) *At the end of the play he ...*

....

....

❸ Using your **own judgement** put a mark along this line to show your attitude towards the Friar based on what you have read.

Not at all sympathetic	A little sympathetic	Quite sympathetic	Very sympathetic
①	②	③	④

PROGRESS LOG [tick the correct box]   Needs more work ☐   Getting there ☐   Under control ☐

Benvolio

❶ Look at this bank of **adjectives** describing Benvolio. Circle the ones you
think best **describe** him:

peaceful	hot-tempered	well-intentioned
kind	sensitive	caring
disloyal	sympathetic	depressed
supportive	volatile	concerned	helpful

❷ Now add a **page reference** from your copy of the play next to each circle,
showing where evidence can be found to **support** the **adjective**.

❸ Complete this **gap-fill paragraph** about Benvolio, adding the **correct information**:

Benvolio is a close friend of Romeo's, and Shakespeare portrays him as a

well-intentioned young man. Benvolio seeks to keep the .... and to

prevent .... He clearly .... for others as he offers to

discover what is upsetting Romeo in order to help Lord and Lady Montague.

He is also a good .... as Romeo chooses to .... his

feelings about Rosaline with Benvolio. Benvolio tries to warn Mercutio that the

hot weather is likely to provoke conflict but Mercutio .... him.

Shakespeare uses Benvolio as a contrast to more aggressive characters like

Mercutio and ....

❹ Write a **paragraph** explaining how **Shakespeare contrasts** the characters of Benvolio and
Mercutio.

....

....

....

....

....

....

PROGRESS LOG [tick the correct box]   Needs more work ☐   Getting there ☐   Under control ☐

Tybalt

❶ Without checking the play, write down from memory at least **two bits of information** that we discover about Tybalt in each of these areas:

His relationship with the other members of the Capulet family	1. 2.
His attitude towards the Montague family	1. 2.
The type of language he uses	1. 2.

❷ Now **check your facts.** Are you right? Look at the following scenes:

a) His relationship with other members of the Capulet family: (I.5.54–92) (III.1.181)

b) His attitude towards the Montague family: (I.1.69–70) (I.5.54–92)

c) The type of language that he uses: (I.1.69–70) (III.1.130)

❸ Write **two sentences** in response to this question: What evidence can we find to show that Tybalt has an aggressive personality?

....
....
....
....
....
....
....
....
....
....
....

PROGRESS LOG [tick the correct box]   Needs more work ☐   Getting there ☐   Under control ☐

Lord and Lady Capulet

❶ **Number** the events below to reveal the changes that can be seen in Lord Capulet's character during the play. Use 1 for the first event and 7 for the final event:

a) Capulet makes peace with Lord Montague.	
b) Capulet insists that Juliet must marry Paris.	
c) At the feast, Capulet avoids conflict when he tells Tybalt not to confront Romeo.	
d) When Paris asks to marry Juliet, Capulet says he will consent to the marriage if Juliet agrees.	
e) Capulet invites Paris to the ball so that he can woo Juliet and win her heart.	
f) When Juliet refuses to marry Paris, he gets angry and calls her a 'baggage' (III.5.160).	
g) He becomes very distressed when Juliet appears to be dead on her wedding day.	

❷ Write **one** or **two** sentences in response to this question:

Why might an Elizabethan audience view Lord Capulet more sympathetically than a modern one?

....

....

....

....

❸ Complete this **gap-fill paragraph** about Lady Capulet, adding the **correct information**:

Lady Capulet thinks that it is appropriate for a woman to marry

for .... Her relationship with Juliet does not seem

as .... as Juliet's relationship with the nurse. She is very

angry when Tybalt dies and asks that the punishment for his murder

should be .... She joins her husband in forcing Juliet to marry

Paris and refuses to .... to her daughter's pleas for help.

She only .... Juliet once she agrees to their marriage

plans. Juliet's death reveals her more .... side.

PROGRESS LOG [tick the correct box]   Needs more work ☐   Getting there ☐   Under control ☐

Lord and Lady Montague

① Look at these **statements** about Lord and Lady Montague and decide whether they are **True [T], False [F]** or whether there is **Not Enough Evidence [NEE]** to make a decision.

a) Lady Montague only appears once in the play.   [T]   [F]   [NEE]

b) Lord Montague does not want to join in the street fight.   [T]   [F]   [NEE]

c) They express their concerns about Romeo to Benvolio.   [T]   [F]   [NEE]

d) Lady Montague is less materialistic than Lady Capulet.   [T]   [F]   [NEE]

e) The Prince does not blame them for the street fight.   [T]   [F]   [NEE]

f) Romeo turns to the Friar, rather than his parents, for help.   [T]   [F]   [NEE]

g) Lady Montague dies from grief when Romeo is banished.   [T]   [F]   [NEE]

② Write **two sentences** in response to each of these questions:

a) How do we know that Lady Montague does not want her husband to fight the Capulets?

....

....

....

....

b) What tells us that Lord Montague cares about his son, Romeo?

....

....

....

....

③ How responsible do you think the Montagues are for the feud?

....

....

....

....

Not at all responsible	A little responsible	Partly responsible	Totally responsible
①	②	③	④

PROGRESS LOG [tick the correct box]   Needs more work ☐   Getting there ☐   Under control ☐

Practice task

❶ First, **read** this **exam-style** task:

Read the passage from *'O God, did Romeo's hand shed Tybalt's blood?'* to *'In such as gorgeous palace!'* (III.2.71–85)

Question: How does Shakespeare present Juliet in this extract?

❷ Begin by circling the **key words** in the **question** above.

❸ Now, complete this table, noting down **three to four key points** with **evidence** and the **effect** created.

Point	Evidence/quotation	Meaning or effect

❹ Draft your response. Use the space below for your first paragraph(s) and then continue onto a sheet of paper.

Start: *In this extract, Shakespeare presents Juliet experiencing a range of emotions. She has just discovered that ...*

....

....

....

....

....

....

....

....

....

PROGRESS LOG [tick the correct box]   Needs more work ☐   Getting there ☐   Under control ☐

Themes

QUICK TEST

❶ Circle the **themes** you think are most **relevant** to *Romeo and Juliet*:

conflict	*light and darkness*	*love*
youth and age	*fate*	*madness*
status	*death*	*time*
religion		*dreams*

❷ Match each of these **characters** with a **theme** from the box above and add a comment about **why** your chosen theme seems **appropriate** to that character:

Lady Capulet   *Tybalt*   *Friar Laurence*   *Romeo*   *the Apothecary*

Character	Theme	Why?
Lady Capulet	*status*	*She is keen for Juliet to advance herself by marrying Paris.*

THINKING MORE DEEPLY

❸ Now choose which you think are **the three most important themes** in
Romeo and Juliet and explain your **reasons in your own words:**

Theme 1: I think Shakespeare wanted to explore the theme of: ....

because ....

....

....

Theme 2: I think Shakespeare wanted to explore the theme of: ....

because ....

....

....

Theme 3: I think Shakespeare wanted to explore the theme of: ....

because ....

....

....

❹ Read the quotations below, and say which theme each one illustrates.
Then, explain in one to two sentences how the quotation illustrates this theme.

a) Romeo : 'And shake the yoke of inauspicious stars' (V.3.111)

Theme: ....

How the quotation illustrates this: ....

....

....

b) Friar Laurence: 'Poison hath residence, and medicine power.' (II.3.20)

Theme: ....

How the quotation illustrates this: ....

....

....

....

5 Some events in the play seem to link to particular themes. What **themes** do these **events** link to, and how are they linked?

a) The reference to the lovers being 'star-crossed' in the first Prologue.

Links to the theme(s) of: ....

....

How they are linked: ....

....

....

b) The servants exchanging insults at the start of the play.

Links to the theme(s) of: ....

....

How they are linked: ....

....

....

c) Romeo and Juliet sharing a sonnet when they first meet.

Links to the theme(s) of: ....

....

How they are linked: ....

....

....

6 What do these quotations from Act II Scene 2 suggest about the nature of Romeo and Juliet's love for each other?

a) Romeo: 'Juliet is the sun!' (II.2.3)

This suggests: ....

....

....

....

b) Juliet: 'I would not for the world they saw thee here.' (II.2.74)

This suggests: ....

....

....

....

EXAM PREPARATION: WRITING ABOUT CONFLICT

Reread the Prologue at the start of the play:

Question: How does Shakespeare use the Prologue to introduce the theme of conflict?

Think about:

- The language Shakespeare uses to describe the conflict between the Montague and Capulet families
- The way he suggests that the conflict will end

7 Complete this table:

Point/detail	Evidence	Effect or explanation
1: *We discover that the family feud has existed for years.*	*'ancient grudge' (line 3)*	*The conflict is likely to be deep-rooted and not easily resolved.*
2: *Shakespeare makes repeated references to conflict using different words to describe it.*		
3: *We discover that the conflict will only end when the lovers die.*		

8 Write up **point 1** into a **paragraph** below in your own words. Remember to include what you infer from the evidence, or the writer's effects:

....

....

....

....

....

9 Now choose one of your other points and write it out as another paragraph here:

....

....

....

....

....

....

PROGRESS LOG [tick the correct box]   Needs more work ☐   Getting there ☐   Under control ☐

Contexts

QUICK TEST ✓

❶ Which of these are **TRUE** statements and which are **FALSE?** Write **'T'** or **'F'** in the boxes:

a) Shakespeare worked as a writer, actor and theatre manager. ☐

b) In the play, Capulet exemplifies (provides an example of) a patriarchal society, one which is ruled by men. ☐

c) It was unusual for couples to marry at a young age in the sixteenth century. ☐

d) An Elizabethan audience often traded and did business during plays. ☐

e) Most people in Shakespeare's time did not believe in God. ☐

THINKING MORE DEEPLY ?

❷ Write **one** or **two sentences** in response to each of these questions.

a) In Shakespeare's time there was frequent political unrest. How do you think this influenced *Romeo and Juliet*?

....

....

....

....

....

b) What is Paris implying when he tells Juliet's father, 'Younger than she are happy mothers made'? (I.2.12)

....

....

....

....

....

c) Why do so many characters seem to respect Friar Laurence?

....

....

....

....

....

It is important to use quotations to support your understanding of the context in which a text was written.

❸ Write **one** or **two sentences** to answer these questions.

a) What does the following quotation tell us about Capulet's attitude to his daughter?

Capulet: 'An you be mine, I'll give you to my friend; / An you be not, hang, beg, starve, die in the streets / For by my soul, I'll ne'er acknowledge thee,' (III.5.192–4)

....

....

....

....

....

b) How does Juliet respond to Capulet's attitude?

....

....

....

....

....

c) What is Sampson's intention when he says:

'I will bite my thumb at them; / which is disgrace to them if they bear it.' (I.1.41–2)?

....

....

....

....

....

d) What are the consequences of Sampson biting his thumb at Abram?

....

....

....

....

....

PROGRESS LOG [tick the correct box]   Needs more work ☐   Getting there ☐   Under control ☐

Settings

❶ Look at the settings diagram below. On the diagram write the names of the characters and events linked to each location. For example, for 'the tomb' you could write 'where Romeo and Juliet kill themselves'.

Verona

Capulet House

Montague House

Streets of Verona

Friar Laurence's cell

Mantua

Adige river

Capulet Family tomb

The Apothecary's shop

THINKING MORE DEEPLY

❷ Write **one** or **two sentences** in response to each of these questions:

a) Why do you think Shakespeare chose Italy as the setting for *Romeo and Juliet*?

....

....

b) How does Shakespeare use the setting of Act II Scene 2 to illustrate the nature of Romeo and Juliet's relationship?

....

....

....

c) What does Juliet imagine she might see in the tomb as she prepares to take the potion? (IV.3.30–50)

....

....

....

❸ Find a word or phrase related to each of these aspects of setting and then explain what the quotation suggests.

a) Verona (the Prologue)

Quotation: ....

What it suggests: ....

....

b) The Italian climate (Act III Scene 1)

Quotation: ....

What it suggests: ....

....

c) Capulet's ball (Act I Scene 5)

Quotation: ....

What it suggests: ....

....

....

PROGRESS LOG [tick the correct box]   Needs more work ☐   Getting there ☐   Under control ☐

Practice task

❶ First, **read** this **exam-style** task:

Question: In the play as a whole, how does Shakespeare present the theme of fate?

❷ Begin by circling the **key words** in the **question** above.

❸ Now, complete this table, noting down **three to four key points** with **evidence** and the **effect** created.

Point	Evidence/quotation	Meaning or effect

❹ Draft your response. Use the space below for your first paragraph(s) and then continue onto a sheet of paper.

Start: *In the play, Shakespeare presents the theme of fate in a range of ways. Firstly, we hear ...*

....

....

....

....

....

....

....

....

....

....

PROGRESS LOG [tick the correct box]   Needs more work ☐   Getting there ☐   Under control ☐

PART FIVE: FORM, STRUCTURE AND LANGUAGE

Form

QUICK TEST ✔

❶ Complete this **gap-fill paragraph** about form, adding the **correct or suitable information**:

Shakespeare wrote thirty-seven .... and these included comedies, histories

and tragedies. Romeo and Juliet *is a tragedy; this means that it deals with loss*

and .... Shakespeare has adapted this form of classical drama, which

is associated with the Ancient .... and Romans. Traditionally a tragedy

would deal with the .... of one high status character but in Romeo and

Juliet *there are two tragic lovers. In classical tragedies death and suffering*

result from a tragic .... in one character but Romeo and Juliet's

deaths act as a punishment for the ....

THINKING MORE DEEPLY ?

❷ Write **one** or **two sentences** in response to each of these questions:

a) What is the dramatic and thematic significance of the Prologue to Act I?

....

....

....

b) In what ways do soliloquies contribute to the drama in *Romeo and Juliet*?

....

....

....

....

c) How could watching a live production of *Romeo and Juliet* improve your understanding of the play?

....

....

....

PROGRESS LOG [tick the correct box]   Needs more work ☐   Getting there ☐   Under control ☐

Structure

QUICK TEST

❶ Match the events below with Shakespeare's dramatic structure.

a) Exposition		**1.**	The lovers die tragically just as the Prologue predicted.
b) Rising action		**2.**	Romeo and Juliet fall in love.
c) Turning point		**3.**	Romeo is banished and Juliet is told to marry Paris.
d) Falling action		**4.**	Mercutio and Tybalt die.
e) Denouement		**5.**	The Prologue sets the scene for the play.

THINKING MORE DEEPLY

❷ Write **one** or **two sentences** in response to each of these questions:

a) Why do you think Shakespeare decided not to include a subplot in *Romeo and Juliet*?

....

....

....

....

....

b) What is the dramatic impact of the action taking place over only a few days?

....

....

....

....

....

c) The Friar's actions have a significant impact on the unfolding events of this play. Which of his actions do you think is the most significant and why?

....

....

....

....

....

EXAM PREPARATION: WRITING ABOUT RESOLUTION

Reread the ending of the play from *'O brother Montague ...'* (V.3.297) to *'Than this of Juliet and her Romeo.'* (V.3.310)

Question: What does the ending of the play reveal about the consequences of Romeo and Juliet's deaths?

Think about:

● The way that Capulet and Montague treat each other

● The language the Prince uses

❸ Complete this table:

Point/detail	Evidence	Effect or explanation
1: *Their deaths bring the feud to an end as the Prologue predicted.*	*'O brother Montague, give me thy hand.' (line 297)*	*Instead of fighting, the rivals are holding out their hands in a gesture of peace.*
2: *The Prince suggests that peace has been achieved at a heavy price.*		
3: *The tragic nature of their deaths is emphasised.*		

❹ Write up **point 1** into a **paragraph** below in your own words. Remember to include what you infer from the evidence, or the writer's effects:

....

....

....

....

❺ Now choose **one** of your other points and write it out as **another paragraph** here:

....

....

....

....

....

PROGRESS LOG [tick the correct box]   Needs more work ☐   Getting there ☐   Under control ☐

Language

❶ First **match** these **words** to their **meanings** without checking the play:

Word:	Meaning:
a) shrift	pilgrim
b) suit	confession
c) visor	went wrong
d) palmer	mask
e) miscarried	request to marry

❷ Now check the **words in context**. Look at the following references. Do you want to change any of your answers?

a) (II.5.77) b) (I.2.6) c) (I.5.24) d) (I.5.100) e) (V.3.267)

THINKING MORE DEEPLY ❓

❸ For each of the **emotions** listed below, think of a moment in the play when it is expressed. Find a **quotation** to back up each of your examples:

Emotion	Moment in the play	Quotation
1: *Anger*	*Mercutio is furious when Romeo refuses to fight Tybalt*	
2: *Love*		
3: *Fear*		

❹ Now **underline** the **key words** in each quotation that convey the **emotion**.

In the play several **literary techniques** are used. Read the **definitions** of these literary techniques:

- **Dramatic irony**: when the audience or a character knows something that the other characters do not.
- **Simile**: when one thing is compared to another using 'like' or 'as'.
- **Metaphor**: when one thing is described as if it really were something else; you do not use 'like' or 'as'.
- **Oxymoron**: when contradictory terms are brought together.

❺ Complete the table below, identifying the technique used in each quotation and giving the meaning or effect.

Example	Literary technique	Meaning/effect
1: *When Romeo describes Juliet as being: ' ... As glorious to this night, being o'er my head / as is a wingèd messenger of heaven' (II.2.26–7)*	Simile	
2: *When Romeo sees Juliet and says, 'What light from yonder window breaks?' (II.2.2)*		
3: *When Romeo refuses to fight Tybalt saying, 'But love thee better than thou canst devise' (III.1.68)*		
4: *When Romeo pines for Rosaline and says, 'O brawling love, O loving hate,' (I.1.176)*		

❻ Blank verse is a type of poetry that does not usually rhyme, but which has a clear pattern of ten syllables in each line. Find one example of blank verse in the play and then find one example of prose (where there is no ten syllable pattern). Write your examples below:

Example 1 (blank verse): ....

Example 2 (prose): ....

❼ In what ways does Shakespeare tend to use blank verse and prose in *Romeo and Juliet*?

....

....

EXAM PREPARATION: WRITING ABOUT LANGUAGE

Reread Mercutio's last words from *'I am hurt.'* (III.1.90) to *'Your houses!'* (III.1.108)

Question: What does Mercutio's use of language reveal about himself and those around him?

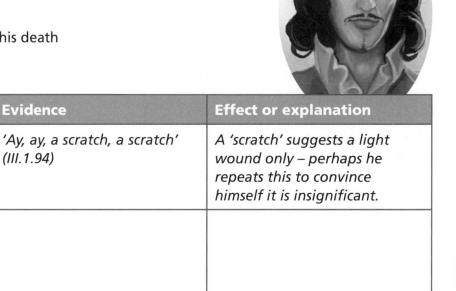

Think about:

- The way he uses puns
- Where he puts the blame for his death

⑧ Complete this table

Point/detail	Evidence	Effect or explanation
1: *Mercutio's light and mocking side is expressed in this attitude to the wound.*	*'Ay, ay, a scratch, a scratch'* (III.1.94)	A 'scratch' suggests a light wound only – perhaps he repeats this to convince himself it is insignificant.
2: *His playfulness and intelligence is expressed despite the reality of the situation.*		
3: *Although he is Romeo's friend, Mercutio's words reveal that he blames both feuding families for his death.*		

⑨ Write up **point 1** into a paragraph below, in your own words. Remember to include what you infer from the evidence, or the writer's effects:

....

....

....

....

....

⑩ Now, choose one of your other points and write it out as another paragraph here:

....

....

....

....

....

....

....

PROGRESS LOG [tick the correct box]   Needs more work ☐   Getting there ☐   Under control ☐

Practice task

❶ First, **read** this **exam-style** task:

Question: How is the language Romeo uses to express his unrequited love for Rosaline different to the language he uses to express his feelings for Juliet?

❷ Begin by circling the **key words** in the question above.

❸ Now complete this table, noting down **three to four points** with **evidence** and the **effect** created.

Point/detail	Evidence	Effect or explanation

❹ **Draft your response**. Use the space below for your first paragraph(s) and then continue onto a sheet of paper.

Start: *At the beginning of the play Romeo is in love with Rosaline but his love is not returned. The language he uses to express this unrequited love is ...*

PART SIX: Progress Booster

Writing skills

❶ How well can you express your ideas about *Romeo and Juliet*? Look at this grid and tick the level you think you are currently at:

Level	How you respond	What your spelling, punctuation and grammar is like	Tick
Higher	● You analyse the effect of specific words and phrases very closely (i.e. 'zooming in' on them and exploring their meaning). ● You select quotations very carefully and you embed them fluently in your sentences. ● You are persuasive and convincing in the points you make, often coming up with original ideas.	● You use a wide range of specialist terms (words like 'imagery'), excellent punctuation, accurate spelling, grammar, etc.	
Mid	● You analyse some parts of the text closely, but not all the time. ● You support what you say with evidence and quotations, but sometimes your writing could be more fluent to read. ● You make relevant comments on the text.	● You use a good range of specialist terms, generally accurate punctuation, usually accurate spelling, grammar, etc.	
Lower	● You comment on some words and phrases but often you do not develop your ideas. ● You sometimes use quotations to back up what you say but they are not always well chosen. ● You mention the effect of certain words and phrases but these are not always relevant to the task.	● You do not have a very wide range of specialist terms, but you have reasonably accurate spellings, punctuation and grammar.	

SELECTING AND USING QUOTATIONS

❷ Read these two samples from students' responses to a question about how Tybalt is presented. Decide which of the three levels they fit best, i.e. **lower** (L), **mid** (M) or **higher** (H).

Student A: *Tybalt is angry when he sees Romeo at Lord Capulet's ball. He asks for a 'rapier' to defend 'the honour of my kin'. His aggressive attitude makes us think that Tybalt wants to fight and kill Romeo.*

Level? ☐   Why? ....

....

Student B: *Shakespeare demonstrates Tybalt's aggressive, volatile nature when he reacts angrily to Romeo's presence at the Capulet ball by demanding 'a rapier'. His eagerness to attack Romeo in a social context indicates that violence is his immediate response to any perceived threat to 'the honour of my kin'. The word 'kin' indicates his wish to protect the reputation of his family.*

Level? ☐   Why? ....

....

ZOOMING IN – YOUR TURN!

Here is the first part of another student response. The student has picked a good quotation but he has not 'zoomed in' on any particular words or phrases:

When the Prince sees that Lord Montague and Lord Capulet have been reconciled after their children's deaths, he says, 'A glooming peace this morning with it brings' which reveals his belief that peace comes at a price.

❸ Pick out one of the **words** or **phrases** the student has quoted and write a further sentence to complete the explanation:

The word/phrase '...' suggests that ....

....

....

....

EXPLAINING IDEAS

You need to be precise about showing that you understand the way in which Shakespeare presents ideas. You can do this by varying your use of verbs (not just using 'says' or 'means').

❹ Read this paragraph from a **mid-level** response to a question about Juliet as she prepares to take the potion. Circle all the **verbs** that are repeated in the student's writing (not in the quotation):

The play shows us Juliet's concerns about taking the potion in the words 'I have a faint cold fear thrills through my veins'. This means that she is frightened and shows that she is in a dangerous situation; it also shows that she is experiencing unpleasant physical sensations as a result of her anxiety which means she is very distressed.

❺ Now choose some of the words below to replace your circled ones:

suggests	*implies*	*tells us*	*presents*	*signals*	*asks*
demonstrates	*recognise*	*comprehend*	*reveals*	*conveys*	

❻ Rewrite your **higher-level** version of the paragraph in full below. Remember to mention the **author by name** to show you understand that he is **making choices** in how he presents characters, themes and events.

....

....

....

....

....

PROGRESS LOG [tick the correct box]   Needs more work ☐   Getting there ☐   Under control ☐

Making inferences and interpretations

WRITING ABOUT INFERENCES

You need to be able to show that you can read between the lines, and make inferences, rather than just explain more explicit 'surface' meanings.

Here is an extract from one student's **very good** response to a question about Romeo's secret meeting with Juliet.

In Act II Scene 2, Romeo visits Juliet in the night by jumping over an orchard wall into her garden. He claims that he scaled the walls 'With love's light wings' suggesting that the power of love has provided him with the physical ability to reach her. The words 'light wings' convey an image of delicate flight, which could be related to birds or angels. Since love, which he personifies, has wings like angels, we could conclude that Romeo's love has a spiritual quality.

❶ Look at the response carefully.

- **Underline** the simple point which explains Romeo's situation.
- **Circle** the sentence that develops the first point.
- **Highlight** the sentence that shows an inference and begins to explore wider interpretations.

INTERPRETING – YOUR TURN!

❷ Read the opening to this student response carefully and then **choose the sentence** from the list which shows **inference** and could lead to **a deeper interpretation**. Remember – interpreting is *not* guesswork!

Lady Capulet is keen for Juliet to marry Paris and encourages her by saying, 'So shall you share all that he doth possess.' This shows that Lady Capulet is clearly thinking about Paris's money. It also suggests that . . .

a) *Paris is the richest man in Verona so Juliet will have an easy life.*

b) *she is revealing how her own attitude to marriage is governed by financial concerns rather than by emotions.*

c) *she is looking forward to a wedding that will have a lot of money spent on it.*

❸ Now complete this **paragraph** about Mercutio, adding your own final sentence which makes inferences or explores wider interpretations:

Mercutio is presented as a lively, cheerful character, and as a close friend of Romeo's. However, he becomes very angry when Romeo refuses to accept Tybalt's challenge. Indeed, Mercutio accuses Romeo of 'dishonourable, vile submission!' This suggests that ... .

....

....

....

....

PROGRESS LOG [tick the correct box]   Needs more work ☐   Getting there ☐   Under control ☐

Writing about context

EXPLAINING CONTEXT

When you write about context you must make sure it is relevant to the task.

Read this comment by a student about Lord Capulet.

Once Capulet decides that Juliet should marry Paris, Shakespeare shows us that he expects Juliet to be 'ruled in all respects' by him. However, we should remember that it would be considered quite normal in a patriarchal society for a father to decide on a husband for his daughter. Therefore, an Elizabethan audience would have understood Capulet's angry reaction to Juliet's disobedience. When Capulet says, 'an you be mine, I'll give you to my friend.' he is implying that Juliet belongs to him and that he has to right to decide her future.

❶ Why is this an effective paragraph about context?

   a) Because it explains how angry Capulet is.

   b) Because it makes a link between Juliet's behaviour and Capulet's furious reaction to it.

   c) Because it tells us how Capulet's attitude towards Juliet was related to the social expectations of the time.

EXPLAINING – YOUR TURN!

❷ Now read this further paragraph, and complete it by choosing a suitable point related to context.

Religion played a significant part in daily life in Shakespeare's time. Romeo and Juliet would have been Catholics. Although some of the characters visit the Friar simply for advice, they would also have been expected to visit him in order to fulfil their religious duties. This is clearly demonstrated when the Nurse says, …

   a) *'Come Lammas Eve …' This shows that the Nurse is aware of the religious calendar.*

   b) *'Have you got leave to go to shrift today?' This shows that Juliet would be expected to go to confession.*

   c) *'God in heaven bless her,' which suggests that references to God and heaven were common at that time.*

❸ Now, write a paragraph about how Shakespeare uses Paris's discussion with Capulet about his marriage proposal to demonstrate the marriage conventions of the Elizabethan era.

Shakespeare shows how … ....

....

....

....

....

PROGRESS LOG [tick the correct box]   Needs more work ☐   Getting there ☐   Under control ☐

Structure and linking of paragraphs

Paragraphs need to demonstrate your points clearly by:

- Using topic sentences
- Focusing on key words from quotations
- Explaining their effect or meaning

❶ Read this model paragraph in which a student explains how Shakespeare presents the character of Benvolio.

Shakespeare presents Benvolio as a peacemaker who tries to prevent conflict. When he tells Tybalt, 'put up thy sword', he is referring to the 'sword' as a symbol of violence. He goes on to suggest that Tybalt should only use his sword as an instrument of peace to part the fighting servants.

Look at the response carefully.

- **Underline** the topic sentence which explains the main point about Benvolio.
- **Circle** the word that is picked out from the quotation.
- **Highlight** or put a tick next to the part of the last sentence which explains the word.

❷ Now read this **paragraph** by a student who is explaining how Shakespeare presents Paris when he visits Juliet's tomb:

We find out about Paris when he says, 'Sweet flower, with flowers thy bridal bed I strew – '. This tells us that he loved Juliet.

> **Expert viewpoint:** This paragraph is unclear. It does not begin with a topic sentence to explain how Shakespeare presents Paris and does not zoom in on any key words that tell us what Paris is like.

Now **rewrite the paragraph**. Start with a **topic sentence**, and pick out a **key word or phrase** to 'zoom in' on, then follow up with an explanation or interpretation.

Shakespeare presents Paris as ... .

....

....

....

....

....

....

....

....

....

It is equally important to make your sentences link together and your ideas follow on fluently from each other. You can do this by:

- Using a mixture of short and long sentences as appropriate
- Using words or phrases that help connect or develop ideas

❸ Read this model paragraph by one student writing about how the Friar is presented:

Shakespeare presents Friar Laurence as a well-respected man. Initially the Friar has some doubts about the sincerity of Romeo's feelings for Juliet, since he was aware of Romeo's previous infatuation with Rosaline, but in the end he agrees to marry Romeo and Juliet, implying that their marriage could bring peace. Later, the Friar shows a weaker side to his character. When he hears footsteps approaching the tomb, he abandons Juliet and runs away for his own safety, which suggests that he fears he may be punished for his role in the unfolding tragedy.

Look at the response carefully.

- **Underline** the topic sentence which introduces the main idea.
- **Underline** the short sentence which signals a change in ideas.
- **Circle** any words or phrases that link ideas such as 'who', 'when', 'implying', 'which', etc.

❹ Read this **paragraph** by another student also commenting on Romeo's parents' concerns about his behaviour:

Romeo's parents discuss their son's recent behaviour with Benvolio. This can be found in Act I Scene 1. They say that Romeo 'Shuts up his windows, locks fair daylight out'. This gives the impression that Romeo is avoiding company. His behaviour seems unusual. He may be depressed.

Expert viewpoint: The candidate has understood how the character's mood is revealed by his actions. However, the paragraph is rather awkwardly written. It needs improving by linking the sentences with suitable phrases and joining words such as: 'where', 'in', 'as well as', 'who', 'suggesting', 'implying'.

Rewrite the **paragraph,** improving the **style,** and also try to add a **concluding sentence** summing up Romeo's behaviour.

Start with the same **topic sentence,** but extend it:

Romeo's parents discuss their son's recent behaviour with Benvolio ... .

....

....

....

....

....

PROGRESS LOG [tick the correct box]   Needs more work ☐   Getting there ☐   Under control ☐

Spelling, punctuation and grammar

Here are a number of key words you might use when writing in the exam:

Content and structure	Characters and style	Linguistic features
Prologue	character	metaphor
Act	role	personification
scene	protagonist	juxtaposition
quotation	dramatic	dramatic irony
sequence	tragedy	repetition
dialogue	aggressive	symbol
climax	humorous	soliloquy
development	sympathetic	euphemism

❶ Circle any you might find difficult to spell, and then use the 'Look, Say, Cover, Write, Check' method to learn them. This means: **look** at the word; **say** it out loud; then **cover** it up; **write** it out (without looking at it!); uncover and **check** your spelling with the correct version.

❷ Create a **mnemonic** for five of your difficult spellings. For example:

tragedy: **t**en **r**eally **a**ngry **g**irls **e**njoyed **d**ancing **y**esterday! Or …

break the word down: T – RAGE – DY!

a) ....

b) ....

c) ....

d) ....

e) ....

❸ Circle any **incorrect spellings** in this paragraph and then rewrite it:

At the start of Act III, the tention builds dramataically as Mercutio and Tybalt fight. This confrontation leads to Mercutio's death and sets the seen for another fight between Tybalt and Romeo. After Romeo kills Tybalt, the audiense watch the tradgedy unfolding as Romeo is banished from Verona.

....

....

....

....

....

....

....

....

④ **Punctuation** can help make your meaning clear. Here is one response by a student commenting on Shakespeare's decision to set the play in Italy. Check for correct use of:

- Apostrophes, full stops, commas and capital letters
- Speech marks for quotations and emphasis

Romeo and Juliet is set in 'fair verona'. Shakespeares audience would probably never have been to Italy but they would know that it was a place with a classical heritage beautiful cities and warm weather. In Act III Scene 1, Benvolio says, The day is hot suggesting that the intense Italian heat might provoke violence.

Rewrite it **correctly** here:

....

....

....

....

....

....

⑤ It is better to use the **present tense** to describe what is happening in the play.

Look at these two extracts. Which one uses tenses **consistently** and **accurately**?

Student A: *Shakespeare told us through the Prologue that the conflict between the Montagues and the Capulets is an 'ancient mutiny'. This emphasised that it had existed for a long time. The romantic relationship between Romeo and Juliet contrasts the hatred of their families. In Act V, due to their deaths, the conflict ended.*

Student B: *Shakespeare tells us through the Prologue that the conflict between the Montagues and the Capulets is an 'ancient mutiny'. This emphasises that it has existed for a long time. The romantic relationship between Romeo and Juliet contrasts the hatred of their families. In Act V, due to their deaths, the conflict ends.*

⑥ Now look at this further paragraph. **Underline** or **circle** all the **verbs** first.

Juliet tried to make her parents understand that she did not want to marry Paris. She pleaded with them not to force her into the marriage. She says, 'I beseech you on my knees'. The use of the word 'beseech' implied that she was begging for mercy. Her parents thought she had been crying about Tybalt and that his death is the cause of her grief.

Now rewrite it using the **present tense** consistently:

....

....

....

....

....

....

....

| **PROGRESS LOG** [tick the correct box] | Needs more work ☐ | Getting there ☐ | Under control ☐ |

Tackling exam questions

DECODING QUESTIONS

It is essential to be able to identify key words in exam tasks and then quickly generate some ideas.

❶ Read this task and notice how the key words have been underlined.

Question: *How does <u>Lord Capulet</u> <u>respond </u>to <u>Paris's request</u> to marry Juliet?*

Write about:

- How Lord Capulet's <u>attitude</u> to the <u>proposal</u> changes as the <u>play progresses</u>
- How Shakespeare <u>presents Lord Capulet</u>

Now do the same with this task, i.e. underline the key words:

Question: *How does Shakespeare convey ideas about death in the play?*

Write about:

- Actual deaths that occur in the play
- Imagery or other language associated with death

GENERATING IDEAS

❷ Now you need to generate ideas quickly. Use the spider-diagram* below and add as many ideas of your own as you can in response to the second question above:

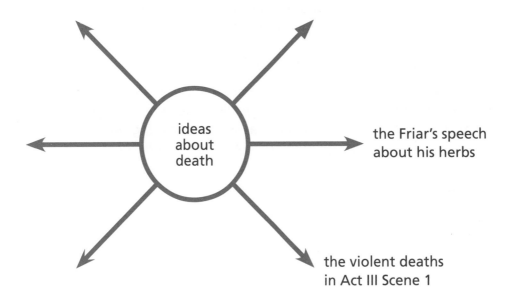

* You can do this as a list if you wish.

PLANNING AN ESSAY

❸ **Using the ideas you generated** in the spider diagram or list for Question 2, write a simple **plan** with at least **five key points** (the first two have been done for you).

a) *The Friar's speech about herbs suggests that death is an everyday part of life.*

b) *The deaths of Mercutio and Tybalt show that conflict results in the senseless loss of young lives.*

c) ....

....

d) ....

....

e) ....

....

❹ Now list **five quotations**, one for each point (the first two have been provided for you):

a) *Friar Laurence: 'Full soon the canker death eats up the plant'.*

b) *Mercutio: 'A plague a'both your houses! They have made worm's meat of me.'*

c) ....

....

d) ....

....

e) ....

....

❺ Now read this task and write a **plan** of your own, including **quotations**, on a separate sheet of paper.

Read from *'Who calls so loud?'* (V.1.57) to *'For there must I use thee.'* (V.1.86).

Question: *How is the Apothecary depicted in this scene and how does Romeo respond to him?*

Start your plan here and continue it on a separate sheet of paper.

....

....

....

....

PROGRESS LOG [tick the correct box] Needs more work ☐ Getting there ☐ Under control ☐

Sample answers   (A01) (A02) (A03) (A04)

OPENING PARAGRAPHS

Here is one of the tasks from the previous page:

Question: *How does Shakespeare convey ideas about death in the play?*

Now look at these two alternate openings to the essay and read the expert viewpoints underneath:

Student A

> *Shakespeare depicts death in a number of ways in Romeo and Juliet. Death seems to be part of everyday life in Verona as the story is set against a background of physical conflict; the violent deaths of Tybalt and Mercutio clearly illustrate this. Throughout the play Shakespeare uses various images associated with death. Most importantly, the tragic deaths of Romeo and Juliet, which are predicted in the Prologue, are realised in the final Act of this play.*

Student B

> *Shakespeare's play is about the deaths of Romeo and Juliet. They fall in love and marry but then Romeo gets banished. Juliet then decides to take a potion that makes her appear dead in order to avoid marrying somebody else. Romeo hears she is dead, rushes to the tomb and kills himself. When Juliet wakes and sees his body she kills herself too.*

Expert viewpoint 1: This is a clear opening paragraph that outlines some of the ideas about death to be discussed. It also suggests that the context of the play has clear connections to this theme. Some specific examples of the images associated with death such as the Friar's herbs and Juliet's fears about waking in the tomb could have been mentioned.

 Mid level

Expert viewpoint 2: This opening recounts the circumstances that lead to Romeo and Juliet dying, without outlining what is to be discussed in the essay, which is the point of the introduction. Other significant deaths and images associated with death need to be mentioned.

 Lower level

❶ Which comment belongs to which answer? Match the paragraph (A or B) to the expert's feedback (1 or 2).

   Student A: ....   **Student B:** ....

❷ Now it's your turn. Write the opening paragraph to this task on a separate sheet of paper:

Read from 'Who calls so loud?' (V.1.57) to 'For there must I use thee.' (V.1 86).

Question: *How is the Apothecary depicted in this scene and how does Romeo respond to him?*

Remember:

- Introduce the topic in general terms, perhaps **explaining** or **'unpicking'** the key **words** or **ideas** in the task (such as 'depict').

- Mention the **different possibilities** or ideas that you are going to address.

- Use the **author's name**.

WRITING ABOUT TECHNIQUES

Here are two paragraphs in response to a different task, where the students have focused on the writer's techniques. The task is:

Read from *'Alas that love, … .'* (I.1.171) to *'Farewell, my coz.'* (I.1.195)

Question: *What techniques does Shakespeare use to show the nature of Romeo's feelings for Rosaline?*

Student A

> *When Romeo speaks about his unrequited love for Rosaline, he says 'O loving hate'. This oxymoron tells us that he is feeling confused. The way Shakespeare makes Romeo speak with contradictions shows us that his feelings for Rosaline are muddled.*

Student B

> *Shakespeare conveys Romeo's feelings for Rosaline by using a series of oxymorons such as 'loving hate', 'heavy lightness' and 'sick health' to express the confused nature of his unrequited love. This type of courtly or Petrarchan love was a popular theme for writers in Shakespeare's time. The fact that Shakespeare includes a large number of oxymorons in Romeo's speech and that these are listed in quick succession suggests that Romeo is caught in a state of confusion between the sweetness of love and the pain of rejection whereby each oxymoron suggests a particular aspect of his condition.*

Expert viewpoint 1: This higher-level response describes the confusion within Romeo's feelings. It also makes connections between the theme of this extract and the wider context of writing in Elizabethan times. It discusses the writer's techniques, using literary terms to good effect. The last sentence is quite long, but nonetheless it links ideas successfully.

Expert viewpoint 2: This mid-level response shows how Romeo's language reflects his feelings. However, the quotation, though appropriate, is not sufficiently embedded in the sentence. There is one reference to the writer's technique and this is not fully explained. In the final sentence the point is not developed.

❸ Which comment belongs to which answer? Match the paragraph (A or B) to the examiner feedback (1 or 2).

Student A: .... Student B: ....

❹ Now, take another **aspect** of Act I Scene 1 and on a separate sheet of paper write your own **paragraph**. You could **comment** on one of these aspects:

- How Benvolio responds to Romeo in this scene
- The language that the servants use in their angry exchanges
- The Prince's judgement after the street fight

⑤ Now read this **lower-level** response to the following task:

Read from 'Who calls so loud?' (V.1.57) to 'For there must I use thee.' (V.1.86).

Question: *How is the Apothecary depicted in this scene and how does Romeo respond to him?*

Student response

> When Romeo visits the Apothecary he calls him 'bare and full of wretchedness,' this means that the Apothecary looks like he is a very poor guy. The Apothecary knows he should not sell poison to Romeo but in the end he has to do it because he really needs the money.
>
> Romeo just cares about getting the poison and he thinks that the Apothecary will sell it to him because he is so poor. Romeo gives the Apothecary some money to get him to sell him a drug so he can commit suicide in Juliet's tomb.

Expert viewpoint: The quotation in the first paragraph is well chosen and gives us a sense of the Apothecary's physical condition, but there is no attempt to embed it in a sentence. Nor is there any real exploration in either paragraph of how Romeo attempts to use the Apothecary's poverty as a means to tempt him into breaking the law and selling the poison. Comments on what Shakespeare intends in this scene are needed, and the language the student uses is sometimes too informal, as in, 'poor guy'.

Rewrite these two **paragraphs**, improving them by addressing:

- The lack of development of linking of points – no **'zooming in'** on **key words and phrases**
- The lack of **quotations and embedding**
- Unnecessary **repetition**, poor **specialist terms** and use of **vocabulary**

Paragraph 1:

In this scene, Shakespeare depicts the Apothecary as ....

....

and also ....

....

This implies that ....

....

Paragraph 2:

Romeo responds to the Apothecary by ....

....

However, ...

....

This suggests that ....

....

A FULL-LENGTH RESPONSE

⑥ Write a full-length response to this exam-style task on a separate sheet of paper. Answer both parts of the question:

Question: *How does Shakespeare depict the Nurse throughout the play?*

Write about:

- How Shakespeare presents her relationship with Juliet.
- How Shakespeare presents her interactions with other characters.

Remember to do the following:

- Plan **quickly** (no more than five minutes) what you intend to write, jotting down **four or five supporting quotations**.
- Refer closely to the **key words** in the question.
- Make sure you comment on **what** the writer does, the **techniques** he uses and the **effect** of those techniques.
- Support your points with **well-chosen quotations** or other evidence.
- Develop your points by **'zooming in'** on particular **words** or **phrases** and explaining their **effect**.
- Be **persuasive** and **convincing** in what you say.
- Check carefully for **spelling**, **punctuation** and **grammar**.

PROGRESS LOG [tick the correct box]   Needs more work ☐   Getting there ☐   Under control ☐

Further questions   (A01) (A02) (A03) (A04)

❶ How does Shakespeare portray the character of the Prince in *Romeo and Juliet*?

❷ Which character(s) do you think are most to blame for the deaths of Romeo and Juliet and why?

❸ Reread the extract from *'Nurse commend me to thy lady …'* (II.4.168) to *'Before, and apace.'* (II.4.211) How does Shakespeare present the older and younger generations in this extract and elsewhere in the play?

❹ Reread the extract from *'My naked weapon …'* (I.1.32) to *'to seek a foe.'* (I.1.80). What is the dramatic significance of the street fight in this extract?

❺ There are several themes in the play, such as love and fate. What do you think is the most important theme and why? (You can write about a theme not mentioned.)

PROGRESS LOG [tick the correct box]   Needs more work ☐   Getting there ☐   Under control ☐

ANSWERS

NOTE: Answers have been provided for most tasks. Exceptions are 'Practice tasks' and tasks which ask you to write a paragraph or to use your own words or judgement.

PART TWO: PLOT AND ACTION [pp. 8–36]

Act I Prologue and Scene 1: Establishing the conflict [pp. 8–9]

1 a) when the lovers die; b) Rosaline; c) death; d) sonnet; e) Romeo

2 a) It shows how bitter the dispute is and establishes the state's concern over the feud.

b) Benvolio is trying to keep the peace whilst Tybalt is actively seeking conflict.

c) Benvolio is determined to find out what is upsetting Romeo.

3

Point/Detail	Evidence	Effect or explanation
1: The Prince thinks the families' behaviour is unacceptable.	'Rebellious subjects, enemies to peace,' (I.1.81)	The adjective 'rebellious' suggests that the families are opposing the state; 'enemies' makes us think of war, adding to the violent tone.
2: He condemns their frequent street fights.	'Three civil brawls, bred of an airy word' (I.1.89)	He shows how angry words quickly become blows and points out that the rival families have caused three street fights.
3: He threatens to punish them.	'If ever you disturb our streets again, / Your lives shall pay the forfeit of the peace.' (I.1.97)	The extreme nature of the proposed punishment shows how annoyed the Prince is about the continuing conflict.

Act I Scene 2: Juliet's future in the balance [pp. 10–11]

1 d) 1; a) 2; e) 3; b) 4; f) 5; c) 6

2 a) Paris respects Lord Capulet and acts courteously towards him but he does try to use persuasion to counter Capulet's concerns that Juliet is too young to marry.

b) If Romeo had not met the illiterate servant he would not have read the guest list for the ball and decided to attend. Therefore, he might never have met Juliet.

c) When Romeo plans to gatecrash the Capulet party he is entering the world of his enemies. His decision to attend the party means that he is destined to meet Juliet and fall in love so that the predictions of the Prologue are fulfilled. It is a meeting which ultimately leads to both their deaths.

3

Point/Detail	Evidence	Effect or explanation
1: Lord Capulet is worried that Juliet may be too young for marriage.	'My child is yet a stranger to this world;' (I.2.8)	The word 'stranger' suggests that she needs more time to experience life before she marries.
2: He is willing to consider Juliet's opinion.	'within her scope of choice / Lies my consent' (I.2.18)	Capulet takes Juliet's feelings into consideration suggesting that he has her best interests at heart.
3: Capulet hopes that Paris can win Juliet's heart.	'But woo her, gentle Paris, get her heart.' (I.2.16)	He seems to want Paris to gain Juliet's affection. He shows no sign at this stage of wanting to force her into marriage.

Act I Scenes 3 and 4: Marriage and misgivings [pp. 12–13]

1 a) F; b) T; c) F; d) F; e) T; f) F; g) T

2 a) If Juliet marries Paris she will share his fortunes so marriage to him will add to her wealth and social status.

b) The Nurse annoys Lady Capulet by talking too much and interrupting her conversation with Juliet.

c) Mercutio tries to lift Romeo's spirits by teasing him, encouraging him to dance and by his witty conversation.

3

Point/Detail	Evidence	Effect or explanation
1: Romeo feels depressed.	'Being but heavy, I will bear the light.' (I.4.12)	The use of the word 'heavy' shows that Romeo feels burdened. It contrasts with 'light', which conveys luminosity and brightness.
2: He refuses to dance.	'I have a soul of lead / So stakes me to the ground I cannot move.' (I.4.15–16)	He feels immobilised by love which links back his previous comment about the heaviness of his feelings.
3: He describes the pain of love.	' ... it pricks like a thorn.' (I.4.26)	This suggests that love can hurt him physically and 'pricks' can also be connected to the idea of Cupid's arrows piercing his flesh.

ANSWERS

Act I Scene 5: Romeo and Juliet meet [pp. 14–15]

1 This scene is set at Lord Capulet's ball. Capulet's nephew, Tybalt, feels **furious** because Romeo is at the party. Capulet does not want Tybalt to **disturb** the party and warns him not to make a **mutiny** amongst his **guests**. He tells Tybalt that he must be **patient** and not challenge Romeo on such an occasion. This shows that Capulet cares about his **reputation** in this context whereas Tybalt always wants to fight with the Montagues, whatever the situation and consequences are.

2 a) Capulet calls Romeo 'virtuous and well-governed' and refers to him as 'portly', which means dignified.

b) Romeo says, 'For / I ne'er saw true beauty till this night' (line 53) and he compares Juliet to light suggesting her radiance.

c) Juliet's mood becomes more troubled when she realises that Romeo is a Montague as she is aware that her family would be angry about any relationship between them. She realises that there might be trouble ahead and that their love could put them in danger.

3

Point/Detail	Evidence	Effect or explanation
1: Romeo and Juliet mirror each other's language.	Juliet: 'And palm to palm is holy palmers' kiss.' Romeo: 'Have not saints lips, and holy palmers too?' (lines 100–1)	The way that they repeat each other's language creates a sense of harmony, for example in the repetition of 'palmers' and the linked 'kiss / lips'.
2: Shakespeare uses religious imagery.	'shrine' (line 94) 'palmers' (line 101)	Religious language conveys the spiritual quality of their love.
3: Romeo shows his devotion to Juliet.	'Good Pilgrim' (line 97)	The central image is of a pilgrim visiting a shrine which shows faith and devotion.

Act II Prologue and Scene 1: More about Romeo [pp. 16–17]

1 a) T; b) F; c) T; d) F; e) T; f) F

2 a) Now that Romeo has met Juliet his life has changed. He needs to be near her. He cannot continue with his life as it was before he met her.

b) Benvolio is anxiously looking for Romeo and worries that Mercutio's remarks will make him angry.

c) Romeo's impetuous behaviour and passionate feelings make Mercutio call him a madman.

3

Point/Detail	Evidence	Effect or explanation
1: The Prologue reminds the audience that Romeo's feelings have changed.	'Old desire doth in his deathbed lie,' (line 1)	Romeo's infatuation is personified as a dying person. The use of the word 'deathbed' foreshadows future events.
2: It sets the scene for future difficulties.	'Being held a foe, he may not have access' (line 9)	This sets the scene for further problems since the word 'foe' means enemy. Juliet's family would oppose any meeting.
3: It shows the strength of Romeo and Juliet's love.	'passion lends them power, time, means to meet' (line 13)	This links to the theme of love and suggests love can overcome difficulties.

Act II Scene 2: The tender meeting of the lovers [pp. 18–19]

1 f) 1; a) 2; c) 3; b) 4; d) 5; e) 6

2 a) sun, moon, stars, daylight, lamp. The references to light indicate Juliet's radiant beauty and they can also be connected to qualities of spirituality and luminosity.

b) She is conscious of the need to marry Romeo quickly before any further plans are made for her marriage to Paris.

c) Juliet is thinking about their names: Capulet and Montague. Since their families are enemies, she suggests that one of them might need to deny or change their name. Her reference to the rose indicates that changing a name does not change the nature or beauty of the flower and therefore if Romeo changed his name he would still retain the same qualities (which she finds attractive).

3

Point/Detail	Evidence	Effect or explanation
1: Juliet's family would kill Romeo if they saw him.	'If they do see thee, they will murder thee.' (line 70)	Romeo's life is in danger because the lovers come from rival families.
2: Romeo has to visit Juliet at night.	'I have night's cloak to hide me from their eyes,' (line 75)	Romeo cannot show his love openly. He has to hide like a criminal. The darkness of night contrasts the light of their love.
3: Juliet worries about the speed of their relationship.	'It is too rash, too unadvised, too sudden' (line 118)	The repetition and the pattern of the phrases suggest she is speaking these words with a sense of rising panic.

ANSWERS

Act II Scenes 3 and 4: Making plans [pp. 20–1]

1 a) herbs; b) peace; c) a challenge; d) he teases her; e) his wedding

2 a) He suggests that the young are too influenced by physical attraction. He also implies that their love is too hasty.

b) The Friar already knows about Romeo's feelings for Rosaline and it is clear that they have discussed these feelings before. This means that Romeo must have consulted him previously.

c) Mercutio means that Romeo seems more like himself because he is cheerful again after the episode when he was miserable and pining for Rosaline.

3

Point/Detail	Evidence	Effect or explanation
1: The Friar uses words related to birth in relation to the natural world.	'mother' and 'womb'	Since life begins in a mother's womb, these words suggest the idea of a baby being born.
2: He also uses words with connotations of death.	'grave' and 'tomb'	Graves and tombs are final resting places for the dead. References to the tomb also foreshadow the final scene where Romeo and Juliet die.
3: The Friar suggests that herbs can cure or kill.	'Poison hath residence, and medicine power.' (line 20)	The herbs are like people as they can do both good and evil. If used in the right hands they heal but used wrongly they can lead to death. This foreshadows the potion Juliet later takes to simulate death and the poison Romeo buys so that he can commit suicide.

Act II Scenes 5 and 6: Waiting and a wedding [pp. 22–3]

1 Juliet is anxious about the passing of **time**. She is waiting impatiently for the Nurse to bring her **news** from Romeo. Juliet is alone on stage as the scene begins, so her speech is a **soliloquy**. She speaks about 'love's **messengers**' and how they should travel as fast as the flickering of the **sun** when clouds pass over it. This image connects to the theme of **light** in the play.

2 a) The Nurse looked after Juliet when she was young so they are close and now the Nurse acts as a confidante and as a messenger between Juliet and Romeo.

b) Juliet seems impatient because she says, 'Loves herald's should be thoughts, Which ten times faster glides than the sun's beams' suggesting that she wants the Nurse to arrive very quickly. Once the Nurse appears Juliet asks her anxious questions and wishes that she could offer the Nurse her healthy bones in exchange for the Nurse's news.

c) The Friar is warning the young couple not to be too hasty because rushing into impetuous actions (even for love) can often end badly. His words foretell the tragic ending of the story where the passionate love and fast moving events of the play lead to the young couple's violent deaths.

3

Point/Detail	Evidence	Effect or explanation
1: Shakespeare suggests that the Nurse is physically weak.	'I am a weary' (line 25)	The Nurse is old and her journey has made her tired, implying a contrast with the vivacity of youth.
2: She seems in no hurry to deliver her news. This implies that she does not fully understand the strength of Juliet's love for Romeo.	'Where is your mother?' (line 56)	This question does not seem to be related to Juliet's questions and could be an example of the Nurse deliberately holding back information or it may be a sign of anxiety about defying her employer. She may be making sure that it is safe to share the news.
3: She does want to help Juliet.	'There stays a husband to make you a wife.' (line 69)	This demonstrates her loyalty to Juliet as she has conspired with her to plan the marriage in secret even though it might put her job at risk.

Act III Scene 1: A fatal fight [pp. 24–5]

1

a) Romeo about Tybalt.

b) Mercutio about Tybalt.

c) Romeo about Juliet.

d) Tybalt about Romeo.

e) Benvolio about Tybalt.

f) The Prince about Romeo.

2 a) Benvolio warns Mercutio that the hot weather is likely to provoke conflict and that the Capulets are in the area, which means that there could be a street fight.

b) Initially, Romeo does not want to fight with Tybalt because Tybalt is Juliet's cousin. Since he loves Juliet, he feels that he should not fight with a member of her immediate family.

c) These words are a pun: grave means serious which contrasts Mercutio's usual playful nature but he also means that he will be in the grave (dead) by the next day.

3

Point/Detail	Evidence	Effect or explanation
1: Romeo's hasty actions have changed his future.	'O, I am fortune's fool!' (line 136).	Romeo realises what he has done and believes he is a victim of fate echoing the Prologue's reference to 'star-crossed lovers.'
2: His mistake must be punished.	'Immediately we do exile him hence.' (line 187)	Romeo is banished not only from his family but also from Juliet. For him this is a fate worse than death.
3: His punishment means that he will never be able to return to Verona.	'Else, when he is found, that hour is his last' (line 195)	He will have to stay away from Juliet or die. Yet, if he is not with Juliet his life will not seem worth living.

Act III Scenes 2 and 3: Dealing with the consequences [pp. 26–7]

1 a) T; b) F; c) T; d) F; e) T; f) F; g) T

2 a) The Nurse promises to go and speak to Romeo for Juliet.

b) Juliet uses a list of oxymorons, in lines 73–80, to describe Romeo. These suggest that she has conflicting feelings about him. She loves him deeply but she is also upset that he has killed her cousin.

c) Romeo feels that his punishment is worse than death since he will be unable to see Juliet. He wants to kill himself.

3

Point/Detail	Evidence	Effect or explanation
1: The Friar stops Romeo from killing himself. However, this intervention just delays Romeo's inevitable death as foretold in the Prologue.	'Wilt thou slay thyself? / And slay thy lady that in thy life lives,' (lines 116–17)	The Friar suggests that Romeo is being hasty and selfish by not thinking about Juliet.
2: He tells Romeo to visit Juliet.	'Go, get to thy love, as was decreed. Ascend her chamber' (lines 146–7)	Romeo will be comforted by the thought of a night with Juliet and by remembering she is waiting for him.
3: The Friar suggests that the Prince might forgive Romeo.	'to blaze your marriage, reconcile your friends, / Beg pardon of the Prince' (lines 151–2)	Here the Friar is giving Romeo hope so that he will stop feeling desperate and believe in the possibility of a better future where the Prince might forgive him.

Act III Scenes 4 and 5: A plan and a parting [pp. 28–9]

1 g) 1; b) 2; c) 3; d) 4; a) 5; e) 6; f) 7

2 a) Juliet feels upset about Romeo's banishment and fearful that she will be made to marry Paris when she is already married to Romeo. This would go against her heart and her religion.

b) Capulet is very angry so he calls Juliet names such as 'baggage' and 'Disobedient wretch'. He threatens to disown her and let her starve on the streets if she will not marry Paris.

c) The Nurse tells Juliet that she should marry Paris even though she knows she has already married Romeo.

3

Point/Detail	Evidence	Effect or explanation
1: Juliet tries to deny that it is morning but Romeo corrects her.	Juliet: 'It was the nightingale and not the lark,' (III.5.2) Romeo: 'It was the lark, the herald of the morn;' (III.5.6)	Juliet attempts to halt time in order to spend longer with Romeo, but he brings her back to reality.
2: Romeo is willing to face danger in order to stay with Juliet.	'Let me be ta'n, let me be put to death.' (III.5.17)	Romeo is in grave danger if he is caught with Juliet but he would accept capture or death to please Juliet.
3: Juliet does not want Romeo to stay and be hurt.	'Then, window, let day in, and let life out.' (III.5.41)	Her mother is approaching so Juliet has to admit that Romeo must leave. When she says 'let life out' she is suggesting that his leaving represents a kind of death to her. Ironically, it is the last time she will see him alive.

Act IV Scenes 1 and 2: Plans and preparations [pp. 30–1]

1

a) Paris about Juliet.

b) Friar about Paris.

c) Friar about Juliet.

d) Juliet about Capulet.

e) Capulet about the Friar.

f) Capulet about Juliet.

2 a) Paris is kind to Juliet but he treats her as if she was already his wife.

b) Lady Capulet is worried about catering for the wedding guests. She thinks they are not prepared enough because they have decided to bring the wedding date forwards.

c) Lord Capulet is happy because he believes that Juliet has repented and regrets her previous disobedience. She seems willing to marry Paris and this is exactly what he wants, as such a marriage will bring her wealth and status.

ANSWERS

3

1: Shakespeare suggests that Juliet is desperate.	'And with this knife I'll help it presently.' (line 54)	Her rash actions mirror Romeo's since he also wanted to kill himself at a time of difficulty.
2: He shows us that she is prepared to face any danger to avoid marrying Paris.	'Chain me to roaring bears,' (line 80)	She lists a number of dangerous acts she is willing to accomplish which could show her bravery or desperation. This indicates to the Friar that she would be willing to take the potion.
3: Juliet has moral concerns about a second marriage.	'without fear or doubt / to live an unstained wife to my sweet love.' (lines 87–8).	The word 'unstained' means 'without sin' as it would be against her religion to get married to Paris when she is already married to Romeo.

Act IV Scenes 3, 4 and 5: The potion ends the wedding plans [pp. 32–3]

1 a) T; b) F; c) T; d) T: e) F; f) F; g) F

2 a) Juliet's lines are filled with questioning as she struggles to control her own imagination. Her questioning develops to include more and more supernatural imagery.

b) The comedy breaks the tension because otherwise we would move straight from Juliet's death to Romeo's plans for his.

c) Juliet's parents and the Nurse are very distressed by her death and this is shown in their language. Shakespeare uses listed, single words, split by commas which might indicate how they are struggling to speak due to grief. Paris also adopts this pattern of speech.

Lady Capulet: 'Accursed, unhappy, wretched, hateful day.' (IV.5.43)

Nurse: 'O woe! O woeful, woeful, woeful day!' (IV.5.49)

Lord Capulet: 'Despised, distressed, hated, martyred, killed!' (IV.5.59)

3

Point/Detail	Evidence	Effect or explanation
1: Shakespeare shows how the Friar stops Juliet's family from expressing their grief.	'Peace, ho, for shame!' (line 65)	He has no reason to grieve, as he knows Juliet is still alive. Their grief may be upsetting him or even making him feel guilty.
2: The Friar appears to reassure Capulet that he should not blame himself for Juliet's death.	'sought ... her promotion' (line 71)	Capulet wanted Juliet to marry Paris to advance her social status but the Friar has reasons to dislike this plan as he had already married her to Romeo.
3: He claims that Juliet is in heaven but the audience know he is lying.	'she is advanced' (line 73)	Here the Friar knows Juliet is still alive and yet he withholds the truth. Perhaps Shakespeare is showing his audience that people who are religious are not always as innocent as they seem.

Act V Scenes 1, 2 and 3: The tragedy unfolds [pp. 34–5]

1 a) Balthasar; b) to see an apothecary; c) Friar John; d) potions; e) Balthasar; f) run away

2 a) Paris seems to show genuine affection and grief as he lays flowers for Juliet. He does not seem to deserve death and even as he dies asks to be placed near Juliet.

b) Everybody involved in the tragedy will feel sorrow about the deaths of Romeo and Juliet. They may not be officially punished but their regret and guilt about the deaths will make them suffer.

c) Although peace has been established it has come at a heavy price since the young lovers have had to die to achieve it. This connects to the themes of conflict, death, love and light.

3

Point/Detail	Evidence	Effect or explanation
1: Romeo uses an image of light to describe Juliet.	'For here lies Juliet, and her beauty makes / This vault a feasting presence full of light.' (lines 85–6)	Death is usually connected to darkness but Romeo continues to refer to Juliet's beauty as illuminating as he has done throughout the play.
2: He claims that Death has not diminished her beauty.	'Death, that sucked the honey of thy breath, / Hath had no power upon thy beauty yet.' (lines 94–5)	Here Shakespeare personifies Death as having stolen Juliet's breath but Romeo feels that Juliet's beauty has defeated Death by remaining intact. This is ironic because he does not realise she is still alive.
3: Romeo wishes to die in order to join Juliet.	'Thus with a kiss I die.' (line 120).	Killing himself is a dramatic action that suggests his devotion to Juliet and his inability to live without her.

PART THREE: CHARACTERS [pp. 37–47]

Who's who? [p. 37]

Left to right: Romeo Montague; Juliet Capulet; Lord and Lady Montague; Lord and Lady Capulet; Friar Laurence; Benvolio; Tybalt; Mercutio; The Nurse

Romeo [p. 38]

1 a) T; b) T; c) NEE; d) T; e) T; f) F; g) F

2 a) From the start of the play, we can infer that Romeo thinks a lot about **love and romance**.

b) When he speaks about his love for Juliet he uses **references to light and religion**.

c) When he needs help, he turns to the Friar because **the Friar is a father figure to him and he represents the authority of the Church.**

d) Romeo's main weakness is that he **acts in haste without thinking about the consequences.**

e) His total devotion to Juliet is demonstrated by **his willingness to die in order to join her in death.**

Juliet [p. 39]

1

Quality	Moments in play	Quotation
a) obedient	When she agrees to consider Paris's proposal	'I'll look to like, if looking liking move.' (I.3.98)
b) impatient	Juliet cannot wait for the Nurse to bring her news	'Love's heralds should be thoughts,' (II.5.4)
c) brave	Taking the potion	'My dismal scene I needs must act alone.' (IV.3.19)
d) loyal	When she kills herself to join Romeo in death	'This is thy sheath; there rust and let me die.' (V.3.170)

2 'I needs must act alone.': Juliet is **isolated** as she is acting without the support of the Nurse.

'What if this mixture does not work at all?': Juliet is **anxious** that the potion will not work.

'No, no, this shall forbid it;': Juliet is **determined** to avoid marrying Paris by taking the potion.

Mercutio [p. 40]

1, 2

lively (I.4.13); witty (II.2.33–41); imaginative (I.4.54–94); light-hearted (I.4.97–9); quick-tempered (I.3.45–8); talkative (III.1.14–29); energetic (1.4.13); bawdy (II.2.33–41)

3 Mercutio is one of Romeo's close **friends.** He provides humour in the play, as his lines are full of **puns.** His 'Queen Mab' speech shows the **imaginative** side of his character. However, Mercutio is not always in a light-hearted mood. He can also be violent and he feels very **angry** when Romeo refuses to fight with Tybalt. Benvolio tries to persuade him to avoid conflict, but Mercutio **ignores** his friend's warning. Mercutio's **death** is a significant point in the play.

4 Mercutio's death is a turning point in the play because Romeo kills Tybalt to avenge it and then gets banished from Verona meaning that he can no longer see Juliet. The absence of Mercutio's humour and energy in the play contributes to the more sombre mood of the final acts.

The Nurse [p. 41]

1

a) 'Thou wast the prettiest babe that e'er I **nursed.**' (I.3.61)

b) 'Enough of this, I pray thee hold they **peace**' (I.3.50)

c) 'O, she is **lame**! Love's heralds should be thoughts,' (II.5.4)

d) 'I am **aweary** give me leave a while.' (II.5.25)

e) 'I think it best you married with the **County.**' (III.5.217)

f) 'She's dead, deceased, she's dead, **alack** the day!' (IV.5.22)

2 a) She adds humour by talking too much and by withholding her message when Juliet is impatient. She also makes sexual references when she speaks about love.

b) Juliet feels betrayed after the Nurse suggests that she should marry Paris.

Friar Laurence [p. 42]

1

a) T; b) T; c) F; d) F; e) NEE; f) T

2 Friar Laurence is a man of holy orders who agrees to marry Romeo and Juliet because he **hopes that their marriage will bring peace.**

Later in the play, he makes further plans to support Romeo and Juliet by **helping Romeo to escape and giving Juliet a potion.**

His plans go wrong when **his letter is not delivered to Romeo.**

He shows that he has a cowardly side when he **abandons Juliet at the tomb.**

At the end of the play he **tells the truth and escapes punishment.**

Benvolio [p. 43]

1, 2

peaceful (I.1.67); well-intentioned (III.1.1–3); kind (I.1.157); sensitive (III.1.1–3); caring (II.2.22); sympathetic (I.1.199); supportive (I.1.157); concerned (II.1.3); helpful (I.1.157)

3 Benvolio is a close friend of Romeo's and Shakespeare portrays him as a well-intentioned young man. Benvolio seeks to keep the **peace** and to prevent **conflict.** He clearly **cares** for others as he offers to discover what is upsetting Romeo in order to help Lord and Lady Montague. He is also a good **listener**, as Romeo chooses to **discuss** his feelings about Rosaline with Benvolio. Benvolio tries to warn Mercutio that the hot weather is likely to provoke conflict but Mercutio **ignores** him. Shakespeare uses Benvolio as a contrast to more aggressive characters like Mercutio and **Tybalt.**

Tybalt [p. 44]

1

His relationship with the other members of the Capulet family	1. Lord Capulet commands him not to upset the party and expects him to obey.
	2. Lady Capulet wants to avenge his death.
His attitude towards the Montague family	1. He is always keen to fight.
	2. He hates all the Montagues.
The type of language he uses	1. He uses aggressive language.
	2. He provokes confrontation.

2 He insists on fighting (I.1.64–6). He overhears Romeo at the ball and has to be stopped from challenging him by Capulet (I.5.54–92). He kills Mercutio and is killed by Romeo in revenge, leading to Romeo's banishment (III.1)

ANSWERS

Lord and Lady Capulet [p. 45]

1 a) 7; b) 4; c) 3; d) 1; e) 2; f) 5; g) 6

2 In Shakespeare's time it was common for a father to make the decisions regarding his daughter's marriage.

3 Lady Capulet thinks that it is appropriate for a woman to marry for **money**. Her relationship with Juliet does not seem as **close** as Juliet's relationship with the Nurse. She is very angry when Tybalt dies and asks that the punishment for his murder should be **death**. She joins her husband in forcing Juliet to marry Paris and refuses to **listen** to her daughter's pleas for help. She only **forgives** Juliet once she agrees to their marriage plans. Juliet's death reveals her more **sympathetic** side.

Lord and Lady Montague [p. 46]

1 a) T; b) F; c) T d) NEE; e) F; f) T; g) T

2 a) She holds him back and tells him 'Thou shalt not stir one foot to seek a foe' (I.1.80).

b) He wants Benvolio to find out why Romeo is unhappy and he defends Romeo when Lady Capulet demands his death after Romeo has killed Tybalt.

PART FOUR: THEMES, CONTEXTS AND SETTINGS [pp. 48–56]

Themes [pp. 48–51]

1 Likely choices: love, conflict, fate, death, light and darkness, religion, time, status

2

Character	Theme	Why?
Lady Capulet	status	She is keen for Juliet to advance herself by marrying Paris.
Friar Laurence	religion	He is a priest, and is well-respected.
The Apothecary	death	He gives Romeo a poison that will kill him.
Romeo	love	Romeo always seems to focus on love. First he loves Rosaline and then Juliet.
Tybalt	conflict	Tybalt is aggressive and actively provokes conflict.

4 a) Fate because 'inauspicious stars' (V.3.111) is a reference to the way that Romeo thinks his destiny is written in the stars. The word 'inauspicious' suggests that fate will treat him badly.

b) Life and death because the Friar's herbs have the potential to both cure and kill.

5 a) The reference to the lovers being 'star-crossed' in the first Prologue.

Links to: fate as it suggests that the lovers' destiny has already been written in the stars.

b) The servants exchanging insults at the start of the play.

Links to: conflict as the servants are deliberately taunting each other and their insults soon lead to a street fight.

c) Romeo and Juliet sharing a sonnet when they first meet.

Links to: love as the shared sonnet creates a sense of harmony and contains religious language suggesting their devotion to each other.

6 a) Romeo: 'Juliet is the sun!' (II.2.46) suggests that Romeo views Juliet as bright and radiant. The words connect to many other instances where he describes Juliet as a source of light.

b) Juliet: 'I would not for the world they saw thee here.' (II.2.74) suggests that Juliet is concerned about Romeo's safety and does not want her family to find him and hurt him.

7

Point/detail	Evidence	Effect or explanation
1: We discover that the family feud has existed for years.	'ancient grudge' (line 3)	The conflict is likely to be deep-rooted and not easily resolved.
2: Shakespeare makes repeated references to conflict using different words.	'mutiny' (line 3) 'foes' (line 5) 'rage' (line 10)	The number of references Shakespeare makes to the conflict reinforces how significant it is.
3: We discover that the conflict will only end when the lovers die.	'Doth with their death bury their parents' strife' (line 8)	This is an example of dramatic irony as we realise the audience already know that the lovers are destined to die but the characters do not.

Contexts [pp. 52–3]

1 a) T; b) T; c) F; d) T; e) F

2 a) His central theme of conflict reflects the turbulent society in which Shakespeare lived, where there were frequent uprisings and plots against the throne.

b) At that time girls often married early and had children at a young age. Paris is implying that Juliet is not too young to marry.

c) In those days people were more religious and the Church was very powerful. The Friar represents the power of the Church.

3 a) This quotation implies that Capulet believes Juliet belongs to him and so he has the right to decide her future.

b) Juliet responds by begging her parents for pity. When this does not work she goes to the Friar and he gives her a potion that will mimic death. Although she is afraid, she takes the potion.

c) Sampson decides to bite his thumb at Abram, as this gesture was considered rude in Shakespeare's time.

d) The consequences are that Abram becomes angry about the gesture, as Sampson intended, and the servants begin to fight. This soon escalates into a wider conflict.

Settings [pp. 54–5]

1 Capulet house: Where Romeo and Juliet meet at the ball and where Juliet later appears on a balcony, speaking to Romeo who stands in the orchard beneath. The Capulet house is also the place where Juliet's parents order her to marry Paris. Juliet takes the potion in her bedchamber in order to appear dead and avoid the arranged marriage.

Montague house: This is where Romeo and his parents live but none of the play's action takes place in this location.

Streets of Verona: The streets of Verona are a place of meetings and conflicts. The rival servants meet and exchange insults here, leading to a street fight. Later, Tybalt and Mercutio die as a result of further conflict on these streets.

Friar Laurence's cell: Romeo visits the cell to ask Friar Laurence to arrange his marriage to Juliet. Later the young couple are secretly married in this location. When Romeo faces banishment and Juliet is ordered to marry Paris, they both go to the cell in order to seek help from the Friar.

The Apothecary's shop: Romeo visits the Apothecary to buy poison so that he can use it to commit suicide beside Juliet's body.

Capulet family tomb: Romeo kills Paris and places his body near to Juliet's in the tomb. Romeo then kills himself so that he can join Juliet in death. When Juliet wakes the Friar tries to persuade her to leave the tomb with him but Juliet refuses to leave and kills herself too.

2 a) As far as we can tell, Shakespeare never travelled abroad but in his day Italy was regarded as a wealthy, romantic country. For Shakespeare's audience, Italy was a place where murderous feuds and passionate love affairs could easily be imagined.

b) Romeo is in a beautiful garden and Juliet is elevated suggesting that Romeo looks up to her. Romeo has to jump the wall to get into the garden showing how he must overcome barriers to reach Juliet.

c) Tybalt's rotting body, bones and skeletons.

3 a) Verona (The Prologue): 'fair' suggests Verona is a beautiful city.

b) The Italian climate (Act III Scene 1): 'the day is hot' suggests that Italy has a hot climate and that this might provoke violence.

c) Capulet's ball (Act I Scene 5): 'musicians play'/'dancing days'/ 'in a mark' suggesting that it was a masked ball with music and dancing.

PART FIVE: FORM, STRUCTURE AND LANGUAGE [pp. 57–63]
Form [p. 57]

1 Shakespeare wrote thirty-seven **plays** and these included comedies, histories and tragedies. *Romeo and Juliet* is a tragedy; this means that it deals with loss and **death**. Shakespeare has adapted this form of classical drama which is associated with the Ancient **Greeks** and Romans. Traditionally a tragedy would deal with the **downfall** of one high status character but in *Romeo and Juliet* there are two tragic lovers. In classical tragedies death and suffering result from a tragic **flaw** in one character but Romeo and Juliet's deaths act as a punishment for the **families.**

2 a) The Prologue is used to comment on the action, provide dramatic irony, overview the plot and introduce key themes such as love, fate and conflict.

b) Soliloquies allow the audience to hear characters' thoughts.

c) Watching a live production of the play would enable you to hear the lines spoken by actors which would give you a deeper understanding of the differences between the characters. The action would happen before your eyes, so you would see the dramatic impact. You could also observe the director's interpretation of the text.

Structure [p. 58–9]

1 a) 5; b) 2; c) 4; d) 3; e) 1

2 a) The absence of a subplot means that the audience's attention is firmly fixed on the fate of the young lovers.

b) The lovers are caught up in a fast-moving series of events beyond their control.

c) Likely answers: marrying Romeo and Juliet because he goes against their parents' wishes and therefore sets the scene for further trouble, giving Juliet the potion because Romeo then believes she is dead and that is why he kills himself.

3

Point/detail	Evidence	Effect or explanation
1: Their deaths bring the feud to an end as the Prologue predicted.	'O brother Montague, give me thy hand.' (line 297)	Instead of fighting the rivals are holding out their hands in a gesture of peace.
2: The Prince suggests that peace has been achieved at a heavy price.	'A glooming peace this morning with it brings,' (line 305)	'Glooming' implies darkness and it contrasts the word 'peace' making us realise the sorrow that underlies the reconciliation.
3: The tragic nature of their deaths is emphasised.	'For never was a story of more woe' (line 309)	Even though the families are reconciled the death of the lovers is mentioned last, giving it a strong dramatic impact.

Language [pp. 60–2]

1 a) shrift — confession
b) suit — request to marry
c) visor — mask
d) palmer — pilgrim
e) miscarried — went wrong

3, 4

Emotion	Moment in the play	Quotation
1: Anger	Mercutio is furious when Romeo refuses to fight Tybalt	'O calm, dishonourable, vile submission!' (III.1.72)
2: Love	Romeo sees Juliet for the first time	'O, she doth teach the torches to burn bright!' (I.5.45)
3: Fear	Juliet is afraid of waking up alone in the tomb	'I have a faint cold fear thrills through my veins' (IV.3.16)

5

Example	Literary technique	Meaning/effect
1: When Romeo describes Juliet as being ' as glorious to this night, being o'er my head / as is a winged messenger of heaven.' (II.2.26–7)	Simile	Romeo is comparing Juliet to an angel.
2: When Romeo sees Juliet and says, 'what light from yonder window breaks?' (II.2.2)	Metaphor	Romeo describes Juliet using a metaphor of light, just like the break of dawn, when he first sees her at the window.

ANSWERS

3: *When Romeo refuses to fight Tybalt saying, 'I love thee better than thou canst devise' (III.1.68)*	*Dramatic irony*	*Romeo does not want to fight Tybalt as he is married to Tybalt's cousin, Juliet. The audience know this but the other characters do not.*
4: *When Romeo pines for Rosaline and says, 'O brawling love, O loving hate,' (I.1.176)*	*Oxymorons*	*Oxymorons consist of pairs of contrasting words which show the bittersweet nature of Romeo's infatuation with Rosaline.*

6 Example of blank verse: Lady Capulet: 'By having him making yourself no less.' (I.3.95)

Example of prose: Gregory: 'The quarrel is between our masters, and us their men.' (I.1.18–19)

7 Blank verse often conveys status whilst characters such as servants usually speak in ordinary prose, which sounds more like ordinary speech.

8

Point/detail	Evidence	Effect or explanation
1: *Mercutio's light and mocking side is expressed in this attitude to the wound.*	*'Ay, ay, a scratch, a scratch' (III.1.94)*	*A 'scratch' suggests a light wound only – perhaps he repeats 'scratch' to convince himself it is insignificant.*
2: *His playfulness and intelligence is expressed despite the reality of the situation.*	*'Ask for me tomorrow, and you shall find me a grave man.' (III.1.98)*	*Even as he dies, Mercutio is speaking in puns. He implies that he will be in the grave (dead) tomorrow but grave also means serious.*
3: *Although he is Romeo's friend, Mercutio's words reveal that he blames both feuding families for his death. His use of repetition underlines this message.*	*'A plague a'both your houses!' (III.1.107)*	*Mercutio repeats this phrase indicating that, in his final moments, he realises that the conflict itself is to blame for his death and not just the Capulets.*

PART SIX: PROGRESS BOOSTER [pp. 66 –77]

Writing skills [pp.64–5]

2 **Student A**: Level – Mid

Why? The student supports what he/she says with evidence and quotations, makes relevant comments and analyses some parts of the text, but the writing could be more fluent.

Student B: Level – Higher

Why? The student analyses the effect of specific words, selects quotations carefully and embeds them fluently in sentences. The writing is persuasive and the points are convincing.

3 The word 'glooming' which is used in association with 'peace' conveys a sense of darkness, which connects to the deaths of Romeo and Juliet and contrasts the images of light which Romeo previously used to express his feelings for Juliet. It means that the peace is tinged with regret.

4, 5, 6

Shakespeare **conveys** Juliet's concerns about taking the potion in the words 'I have a faint cold fear thrills through my veins'. This **suggests** that she is frightened and shows that she is in a dangerous situation; it also **implies** that she is experiencing uncomfortable physical sensations as a result of her anxiety which **tells us** she is very distressed.

Making inferences and interpretations [pp. 66–7]

1 **In Act II Scene 2, Romeo visits Juliet in the night by jumping over an orchard wall into her garden. He claims that he scaled the walls 'With love's light wings' suggesting that the power of love has provided him with the physical ability to reach her.** The words 'light wings' convey an image of delicate flight which could be related to birds or angels. **Since love, which he personifies, has wings like angels, we could conclude that Romeo's love has a spiritual quality.**

2 b)

Writing about context [p. 67]

1 c)

2 b)

Structure and linking of paragraphs [p.68]

1 **Shakespeare presents Benvolio as a peacemaker who tries to prevent conflict.** When he tells Tybalt, 'put up thy sword', he is referring to the **'sword'** as a **symbol of violence**. He goes on to suggest that Tybalt should only use his sword as an instrument of peace to part the fighting servants.

2 **Shakespeare presents Friar Laurence as a well-respected man.** Initially the Friar has some doubts about the sincerity of Romeo's feelings for Juliet, since he was aware of his previous infatuation with Rosaline, but in the end he agrees to marry Romeo and Juliet, **implying** that their marriage could bring peace. **Later, the Friar shows a weaker side to his character. When** he hears footsteps approaching the tomb, he abandons Juliet and runs away for his own safety, **which** suggests that he fears he may be punished for his role in the unfolding tragedy.

Spelling, punctuation and grammar [pp. 70–1]

3 At the start of Act III, the **tension** builds **dramatically** as Mercutio and Tybalt fight. This confrontation leads to Mercutio's death and sets the **scene** for another fight between Tybalt and Romeo. After Romeo kills Tybalt, the **audience** watch the **tragedy** unfolding as Romeo is banished from Verona.

4 *Romeo and Juliet* is set in 'fair **Verona**'. **Shakespeare's** audience would probably never have been to Italy but they would know that it was a place with a classical heritage, beautiful cities and warm weather. In Act III Scene 1, Benvolio says, 'The day is hot ...' suggesting that the intense Italian heat might provoke violence.

5 **Student B**

6 **Verb tenses marked in original text**

*Juliet **tried** to make her parents understand that she **did** not want to marry Paris. She **pleaded** with them not to force her into the marriage. She **says**, 'I beseech you on my knees'. The use of the word 'beseech' **implied** that she was begging for mercy. Her parents **thought** she **had** been crying about Tybalt and that his death **is** the cause of her grief.*

7 Corrected version

*Juliet **tries** to make her parents understand that she **does** not want to marry Paris. She **pleads** with them not to force her into the marriage. She **says**, 'I beseech you on my knees'. The use of the word 'beseech' **implies** that she **is** begging for mercy. Her parents **think** she **has** been crying about Tybalt and that his death **is** the cause of her grief.*

Tackling exam questions [pp. 72]

4, 5

c) The Apothecary sells Romeo a poison which he can use to commit suicide even though this is against the law. However, Romeo believes that the poison is a good thing, as it will enable him to die and therefore join Juliet in death.

'Come cordial and not poison, go with me

To Juliet's grave. For there must I use thee.' (V.1.85–6)

d) The tomb, a symbol of death, is the setting for the deaths of Paris, Romeo and Juliet. Yet when Romeo sees Juliet in the tomb he claims that death has not diminished her.

'Death, that hath sucked the honey of thy breath,

Hath no power yet upon thy beauty' (V.3.93)

e) Shakespeare shows how the tragic deaths of Romeo and Juliet finally bring an end to the conflict between their families just as the Prologue predicted.

'As rich shall Romeo by his lady's lie,

Poor sacrifices for our enmity!' (V.3.303–4)

Sample answers [pp. 74–7]

1 Student A: Expert viewpoint 1; Student B: Expert viewpoint 2

3 Student A: Expert viewpoint 2; Student B: Expert viewpoint 1